THE OPTION
TRADER'S HEDGE
FUND

THE OPTION TRADER'S HEDGE FUND

A BUSINESS FRAMEWORK FOR TRADING EQUITY AND INDEX OPTIONS

Dennis A. Chen

Mark Sebastian

Vice President, Publisher: Tim Moore
Associate Publisher and Director of Marketing: Amy Neidlinger
Executive Editor: Jim Boyd
Editorial Assistant: Pamela Boland
Operations Manager: Jodi Kemper
Assistant Marketing Manager: Megan Graue
Cover Designer: Chuti Prasertsith
Managing Editor: Kristy Hart
Project Editor: Betsy Harris
Copy Editor: Cheri Clark
Proofreader: Debbie Williams
Indexer: Larry Sweazy
Senior Compositor: Gloria Schurick
Manufacturing Buyer: Dan Uhrig

© 2012 by Dennis A. Chen and Mark Sebastian

Published by Pearson Education, Inc.
Publishing as FT Press
Upper Saddle River, New Jersey 07458

This book is sold with the understanding that neither the author nor the publisher is engaged in rendering legal, accounting, or other professional services or advice by publishing this book. Each individual situation is unique. Thus, if legal or financial advice or other expert assistance is required in a specific situation, the services of a competent professional should be sought to ensure that the situation has been evaluated carefully and appropriately. The author and the publisher disclaim any liability, loss, or risk resulting directly or indirectly, from the use or application of any of the contents of this book.

FT Press offers excellent discounts on this book when ordered in quantity for bulk purchases or special sales. For more information, please contact U.S. Corporate and Government Sales, 1-800-382-3419, corpsales@pearsontechgroup.com. For sales outside the U.S., please contact International Sales at international@pearsoned.com.

Company and product names mentioned herein are the trademarks or registered trademarks of their respective owners.

Printed in the United States of America

ISBN-10: 0-13-480752-9
ISBN-13: 978-0-13-480752-2

Pearson Education LTD.
Pearson Education Australia PTY, Limited.
Pearson Education Singapore, Pte. Ltd.
Pearson Education Asia, Ltd.
Pearson Education Canada, Ltd.
Pearson Educación de Mexico, S.A. de C.V.
Pearson Education—Japan
Pearson Education Malaysia, Pte. Ltd.

Library of Congress Cataloging-in-Publication Data

Chen, Dennis A. (Dennis Anthony), 1970-

   The option trader's hedge fund : a business framework for trading equity and index options / Dennis A. Chen, Mark Sebastian.

    p. cm.

   Includes index.

   ISBN 978-0-13-282340-1 (hardcover : alk. paper) -- ISBN 0-13-282340-3

   1. Options (Finance) 2. Portfolio management. 3. Risk management. I. Sebastian, Mark, 1978- II. Title.

   HG6024.A3C4852 2012

   332.64'524--dc23

                         2012007222

For Melinda,
Thank you for encouraging me and standing by me
in all of our endeavors.

For my partners at Smart Income Partners, Ltd.,
Thank you for your trust and support. Thank you for believing and
investing in our business.
—Dennis

To Lauren, thank you for putting up with me through thick and thin;
without you all of this is nothing.

To my parents, thank you for pushing me to constantly try to exceed
expectations and never settle.

To my son, may the road that lies ahead be all you could hope for.

To my partner, co-workers, and all of those associated with Option Pit,
thank you for making what I do not seem like work.
—Mark

Contents

Part III Lessons from the Trading Floor

Foreword

As Director of Research and Co-Portfolio Manager of Jim Cramer's Charitable Trust, I continuously look for more effective ways to oversee the fund and improve returns. Although it is a long-only equity fund, it is imperative to have a working knowledge of all asset classes and their effects on the broader market and trading psychology. One of the most impactful metrics of managing money in today's market is, without question, volatility.

Volatility as an asset class is a rapidly growing concept in the marketplace. Indexes and products have been introduced to trade, hedge, and use as forecasting mechanisms.

Financial media commonly portrays the VIX, or CBOE Volatility Index, as an indication of "fear" in the market. Typically, when the VIX is trading higher, stocks are moving lower and the inverse applies. Yet it is far more important than that, as the VIX and volatility-based products have brought the market to its next stage of evolution.

The Chicago Board Options Exchange began its academic work on the VIX in the early 1990s. Today's index has evolved into a product with futures and options contracts based on the S&P 500, which allows for a more accurate view of investors' expectations on future market volatility. Following the financial meltdown in the back half of 2008, implied volatility exploded as the market imploded, and that is when market participants embraced volatility as a diversification tool. Other exchanges have now developed their own futures and derivatives products across multiple asset classes and commodities, including currency, gold, and oil.

Mark Sebastian is truly a master of trading options and futures on volatility derivatives. When it comes to the technical subtleties of complicated markets, his analysis and ability to break down the mathematical and quantitative complexities in an intelligent and understandable style is second to none. Mark forces you to think in different ways about the option and futures markets, often in ways that are outside the comfort zone.

For this book, Mark joined forces with his friend Dennis Chen and convinced him to share the framework and processes used when managing his hedge fund. By doing so, they provide you with a real-world perspective to the business of trading options.

Albert Einstein said, "Any intelligent fool can make things bigger, more complex, and more violent. It takes a touch of genius—and a lot of courage—to move in the opposite direction." Mark and Dennis's uncanny way to consistently come up with out-of-the-box strategies encourages traders to dig deep and really understand the world of derivative-based products. From my perspective, Mark and Dennis's ideas, strategies, framework, and concepts are sophisticated yet easy to understand and implement, which is invaluable when trying to beat the competition and the broader averages.

The Options Trader's Hedge Fund is a unique tool that carefully explains how traders can effectively identify and manage positions like the top volatility experts do using key strategies in trend, time, and volatility. As unique as its authors, it encourages investors to embrace their individuality when developing a trading plan and discipline for trading options.

A captivating and masterful read, *The Options Trader's Hedge Fund* is a must-have guide that every professional trader should have in his or her library. The biggest takeaways center on methodology, risk control, and effective use of capital—the cornerstones for successful money management and trading.

Trade well,

Stephanie Link
Director of Research, Co-Portfolio Manager, & VP of Strategy
The Street

Acknowledgments

This book is the result of a set of experiences that we have collected over the years. Whether knowingly or unknowingly, many people and organizations have directly and indirectly helped shape the content of *The Option Trader's Hedge Fund*. We would like to thank the following people and organizations for sharing with us experiences that helped create this book:

- Adam Paris, Cofounder of the OptionPit.com
- Alexander Elder, Trading Coach and author of *Trading for a Living*
- Jim Boyd, Executive Editor, FT Press
- Cheri Clark, Copy Editor, FT Press
- Betsy Harris, Project Editor, FT Press
- Harry Strachan, Partner at Bain & Co. and Mesoamerica Partners
- Jeremy Siegel, Finance Professor at the Wharton School and author of *Stocks for the Long Run*
- Kerry Lovvorn, Trading Coach
- Livevol
- OptionVue
- Paul Hayward, Michael Shore, Nina Yoo, and the CME Group's Corportate Communications team
- Robbie Garcia, Cofounder, Smart Income Partners, Ltd.
- Robert Walberg, Stephanie Link, Jill Malandrino, and The Street
- Shawn and Shelly Howton, Professors at Villanova
- The Chicago Mercantile Exchange

- The Chicago Board Options Exchange
- The Options Institute
- The team at FT Press who assisted in the production of this book
- TD Ameritrade and ThinkorSwim

About the Authors

Dennis A. Chen is a hedge fund manager, investor, management advisor, and entrepreneur. He is the founder and Chief Investment Officer of Smart Income Partners, Ltd., a hedge fund specializing in generating income using index and equity options. Dennis has been investing and trading equities and options for many years. He has previously served as a management consultant at Bain & Company where he focused on financial services (banking and insurance). He was a principal at Diamond Technology Partners, Inc. As an entrepreneur, Dennis has purchased, improved, and sold several small businesses. He has experience in multiple industries, including banking, insurance, real estate, computer technology, Internet, publishing, advertising, construction, commodities, quick-service restaurants, and automotive. His broad business experience enables him to make better investment decisions at his hedge fund. Dennis earned his MBA from The Wharton School of Business. He also holds a Master's in Computer Science from Arizona State University and a Bachelor's degree in computer science from the University of Texas.

Mark Sebastian is a former member of both the Chicago Board Options Exchange and the American Stock Exchange. He is the Chief Operating Officer of Option Pit Mentoring and Consulting, a Chicago-based option education firm. Sebastian has been published nationally on Yahoo! Finance and has been quoted in *The Wall Street Journal*, Reuters, Bloomberg, and on Jim Cramer's *Mad Money* show on CNBC. He has appeared on CNBC, Fox Business, and Bloomberg. He is an "all-star contributor" for The Street's Option Profits Team. Mark is also the Managing Editor for *Expiring Monthly: The Option Traders Journal* digital magazine focused exclusively on options trading. He has spoken for the CBOE, the ISE, CME, and VOLX; is a co-host on the popular *Option Block* podcast; and the *Volatility Views* podcast. Mark has a Bachelor's of Science in finance from Villanova University.

Preface

The idea of this book began in Las Vegas in 2010. Mark and I were attending a conference and we were working on growing our respective businesses. Mark is the founder, COO, and Director of Education at OptionPit.com. He is a former market maker at the CBOE and AMEX. He has appeared on CNBC, Fox Business, and Bloomberg. He has also been quoted in *The Wall Street Journal* and is a featured contributor at Option Profits of TheStreet.com. He is an expert in the field of options trading. On the other hand, I am more of a behind-the-scenes guy. I operate more like a KGB or CIA operative. Up to now, you would have known what I have been doing only if you were a partner at my hedge fund. I trade options for a living. I am the co-founder and Chief Investment Officer of Smart Income Partners, Ltd., a hedge fund that trades options to generate consistent income for its partners. I earned an MBA from The Wharton School. I have experience in many different businesses, including financial services and insurance, that I gained as a management consultant at Bain & Co. and as an entrepreneur.

Mark and I share a passion for trading options profitably. We have read many books on options and options trading. Most of them answer the question of "what" options are. They are very descriptive and provide useful information. However, rarely do you find a book that answers the question of "how" to make money in an option trading business. How do you develop the framework for an option trading business? How do you implement a system? How do you actually trade? How do you make money consistently? How do you build a business out of trading options?

Given that void, we decided to write this book. We believe that we bring a different perspective to the business of trading options. This book brings you our combined experiences to help you build a successful option trading business. We will show you the "how-to" and give you a framework in which to operate. The book is based on the way I manage Smart Income Partners, Ltd. Smart Income Partners is a hedge fund that specializes in trading options to generate consistent monthly income for its partners. The fund is managed exactly like an insurance company.

It uses the business model of an insurance company. In this book we will share with you the concept of The One Man Insurance Company (TOMIC). TOMIC is the business framework that is used at Smart Income Partners, Ltd.

The book also offers insights drawn from the vast experience in trading options that Mark has had as market maker at the CBOE and NYSE. Mark also draws from all his experiences from coaching students at OptionPit.com. I must say, not because he is my friend and co-author, that Mark provides one of the best option coaching programs available today. I highly recommend OptionPit.com, where I personally am subscribed as a professional member. Mark is consistently thought provoking, and he pushes the envelope on option trading. You may refer to Appendix C, "OptionPit.com," for an overview of OptionPit.com services.

I must warn you, this book should not be your first book in dealing with the options world. It is worthwhile if you have a working knowledge about options or if you currently trade options. If you are a novice in trading options, we suggest you read some other primers on options before reading this book. Readers will benefit most if they have some knowledge of options.

A small but necessary disclaimer: *The Option Trader's Hedge Fund* is intended for educational purposes only. The book reflects the philosophy of how Smart Income Partners is managed. However, due to regulatory restrictions, this book does not share any performance information about Smart Income Partners, Ltd., and is not intended to solicit any business for the hedge fund. The fund is offered only to qualified investors on a one-on-one basis through a private placement memorandum. If you would like information about Smart Income Partners, Ltd., you may contact me directly at dchen@smart-advisors.com.

Mark and I want to thank you in advance for taking the time to read this book. We hope this book will help you build a profitable option portfolio.

Dennis A. Chen
January 2012

Introduction

The world of investments is very large. You can invest in stocks, bonds, options, real estate, CDs, commodities, or futures. Regardless of where you choose to invest your money and time, it would be very wise to have a framework with which to manage your investments. This book suggests a framework for trading options profitably; this framework has been used by an option trading hedge fund. The book is a road map for anyone wanting to trade options. We provide guidelines on how to run an option trading business successfully. We also provide you with our own experiences, learned along the way as a professional hedge fund manager (Dennis Chen) and a former market maker and trading coach (Mark Sebastian).

If you are reading this book, you already may have experienced trading options. We will not teach you how to set up a hedge fund or how to invest in hedge funds. There are other books to help you set up a hedge fund if you so desire. This book gives you a glimpse of how a particular hedge fund, Smart Income Partners, Ltd., successfully trades options for its partners. Smart Income Partners, Ltd., is an option trading hedge fund managed by Dennis Chen, a co-author of this book.

At his hedge fund, Dennis views trading options in a different light. He thinks of his business not as a hedge fund, but as an insurance company. When asked the question "What do you do for a living?" most hedge fund managers would say, "I manage a hedge fund," or "I'm a money manager." When someone asks Dennis what he does for a living, he answers, "I manage risk for a financial insurance company." Let us introduce to you the concept of "The One Man Insurance Company," or TOMIC. TOMIC is the business framework Dennis uses to operate and guide his hedge fund. TOMIC is a framework that anyone could use to manage their option portfolio. You too could run The One Man Insurance Company. In the following pages we introduce the concept, explain the framework, and show you how to manage your option trading business like Dennis does at his hedge fund. Also, you will find throughout the book key lessons they have learned during their trading careers.

Part I of the book, "The Framework," shows you the framework details of TOMIC.

Chapter 1, "The Insurance Business," provides an overview of the insurance business and compares it to the way the hedge fund thinks about its option trading operations. You will review the value chain of a traditional insurance company and compare it to the value chain of The One Man Insurance Company. You will learn what key success factors are needed to run a successful TOMIC. You will gain a better understating of the business of TOMIC.

Chapter 2, "Trade Selection," provides you with guidelines of trades chosen for TOMIC. You will learn about market selection, direction, timing, volatility, and pricing. Each of these five factors impact your trade selection, which is the underwriting function at TOMIC. It is the key to making money trading options.

Chapter 3, "Risk Management," reviews the risks taken at TOMIC and how to manage those risks to avoid a terminal loss of the business. This chapter discusses position sizing, money management, diversification, protection against "black swan" events,[1] and trade exits.

Chapter 4, "Trade Execution," explains how to implement the trades you place. It shows how to get them done efficiently. This chapter gives you a better understanding of the conditions to look for before placing the trade and how to place the trade in order to get better fills.

Chapter 5, "The Trading Plan," discusses the importance of having a plan, and it reviews the process of creating your trade plan.

Chapter 6, "Trading Infrastructure," reviews all the tools and services you need in order to be able to run a successful option trading business.

Chapter 7, "Learning Processes," reviews the importance of a feedback loop. We include suggestions on supporting functions necessary to maintain the edge in the business of trading options.

In Part II of the book, "Implementing the Business," we give you a taste of how to implement the business. This part of the book shows you specific examples of different trades that are used at the hedge fund that you could implement in your TOMIC. You will see how to trade a vertical spread, an iron condor, a butterfly, a calendar spread, and a ratio spread.

Chapter 8, "Understanding Volatility," shows you what you need to know about volatility to implement the TOMIC.

Chapter 9, "Most Used Strategies," shows you in detail the five most frequently used strategies at TOMIC. It provides you with the key criteria for using each strategy.

Chapter 10, "Operating the Business: Putting Together TOMIC 1.0 from A to Z," provides guidelines for creating TOMIC 1.0. It provides you the answer to how to create your own TOMIC.

Part III, "Lessons from the Trading Floor," is a selection of blogs written by Mark Sebastian for OptionPit.com, with an occasional guest blog written by Dennis Chen. The section covers lessons learned at the option pits on different topics. You will find words of advice on risk management, volatility, trading and execution, and the Greeks.

Once you have finished reading this book, you will have a good understanding of the insurance company framework used to build a profitable option portfolio. As you build your option trading business, you might decide to read the book again because there are additional insights you will get after you've experienced real trading conditions. The markets are constantly changing. We encourage you to continuously learn and seek to improve your trading every day. This book was written to be a guide, but you must walk your own path.

Endnote

1. A black swan event is an unexpected event of large magnitude and consequence. The black swan theory was developed by Nassim N. Taleb. Refer to his book *The Black Swan*.

1

The Insurance Business

In this chapter we show you how to create a business of trading options successfully by using the framework of an insurance company. This is the same framework used at a hedge fund managed by Dennis (the co-author of this book). So, for this book, we create the concept of The One Man Insurance Company (TOMIC). You will need to know how the insurance business works. What is the good, the bad, and the ugly of the insurance business? How does an insurance company make money? How does it lose money? What are the key profit drivers of the business, and what are the key success factors?

Insurance is the equitable transfer of risk from one entity to another in exchange for compensation, called a premium. The insurance companies make money by taking risks from others in exchange for a premium. For example, if you own a vehicle, you probably have car insurance that protects your asset against a big loss like theft or accident. The insurance company collects a premium each year to protect you against the big loss. The insurance company pays you to make you whole. For an insurance company to function, it must know what risks it is willing to insure. It also needs to know how much premium it needs to charge to be able to back the risks and still earn a profit. It will need to know the car-theft statistics and accident statistics for your car's model and year. Using that information, the company is able to price coverage and charge a premium that allows the company to make a profit on the large pool of car insurance it writes.

Figure 1.1 illustrates a generic value chain of an insurance company.

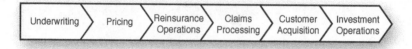

Figure 1.1 Insurance company value chain.

The main functions in an insurance company are these:

- Underwriting: Defining and selecting risks to insure
- Pricing: Identifying the insurance premium for the risk taken
- Reinsurance: Divesting or redistributing unwanted risk
- Claims processing: Dealing with customers and payout of insurance losses
- Customer acquisition: Selling insurance policies
- Investment operations: Earning additional income on reserves (float)

The underwriting function selects risks the insurance company is willing to insure. This function defines characteristics of the risk and analyzes the statistical outcomes of the risk. For example, the underwriting function of a property and casualty insurance company would look at the auto insurance market and decide which segment of the market they would like to insure. The underwriters, through their analysis, may find out that the small-SUV segment driven by married women between the ages of 24 and 36 have only a 1% chance of an accident versus the general average SUV accident rate of 5%. The underwriters may decide that this is a segment they would like to have in their portfolio of insurance policies.

The pricing function determines the amount of premium to charge for the risk being insured. Continuing this example, the insurance company prices the small SUV driven by married women between ages 24 and 36 at a price that generates a positive expected return. They price it at an expectation of a 20% return on premiums written for the year.

The reinsurance operation divests or relocates unwanted risk. The insurance company buys insurance from other insurance companies or reinsurance companies to spread risk among many. In effect, it transfers the unwanted risk to other entities (reinsurance companies) that are willing to bear the unwanted risks in exchange for compensation. An example of this is a property and casualty insurance company (Auto Insurance Co.) with a large base of auto insurance subscribed in the San Francisco Bay Area. The company is not willing to take the risk of an earthquake wiping out all the insured vehicles. Auto Insurance Co. is comfortable insuring the vehicles for normal accidents and theft, but if the Big One (earthquake) happens it will cause damage to all the company's insured cars. Therefore, the insurance company reinsures earthquake risk by buying earthquake insurance from a reinsurance company (let's call it Reinsurance Co.) that specializes in catastrophic insurance and is willing to assume the earthquake risk. So, if the Big One hits, Auto Insurance Co. would not lose because Reinsurance Co. would pay the Auto Insurance Co. for the earthquake claims, which in turn uses the funds to pay the individual auto claims. Hence, its risk of an earthquake was undertaken by the reinsurer and not the auto insurance company.

The claims processing function determines the cost of a loss and pays claims to the insured. Going back to the auto insurance company example, the claims processing unit sends out adjusters to an accident to evaluate the loss and to start the claim process. This involves customer service as well as compensation since the adjuster deals with the insured and wants to provide good service in order to keep them as a client.

The customer acquisition function is executed through agents and brokers. They are responsible for selling the insurance policies. The agents may be exclusive agents or outside agents. The channels could be through physical agencies (offices), by phone, or online (using the Internet). This function is also supported by marketing and customer service departments.

The investment operation function is a profit center of an insurance company. There are two types of profits generated in insurance: underwriting profits and investment profits. The underwriting profits are generated directly from writing insurance policies. Underwriting profits are what is left after the premiums are collected and claims are paid. The investment profits are generated from investing the premiums and reserves set up when policies are written. Some people refer to investment profits as income generated from the "float" on the insurance companies. Warren Buffett is a master at investing. The insurance businesses in Berkshire Hathaway (GEICO and General Re, for example) are required to create a set amount of reserves. These reserves are invested by Warren Buffett to generate income. This is the income derived from the investment operations.

How Insurance Companies Make Money

Insurance companies make money from underwriting and from operations. Underwriting profits come from selling insurance and taking on risks. Investment profits are profits in the form of investment returns. TOMIC makes almost all of its money from underwriting operations. TOMIC could make money from investments also, but this topic is not covered in this book.

Here is an example of how an insurance company makes money selling automobile insurance. Each year ABC Auto Insurance Co. insures 10,000 cars with average value of $20,000 per car, and it charges on average $1,000 annual premium for each car. Each year it has on average 1,000 claims where the average cost of a claim is $4,500. Looking at the insurance operations, ABC Auto Insurance Co. earns a profit of $5,500,000.

This is how a gross Profit and Loss summary looks:

Earned Premium = $10,000,000; 10,000 cars × $1,000 premium

Incurred Loss = ($4,500,000); 1,000 claims × $4,500 cost of claim

Profit = $5,500,000; Profit from insurance under writing operations

Of course, there will be administrative overhead beyond this gross profit. Also, while ABC is waiting to pay out claims, it makes more profit from investing the money it collects as premiums and earns investment income. So, assuming ABC can earn about 3% on the premiums it collected and it maintained an average float (premium collected and not paid out as claims) of $2,750,000 ($5,500,000/2), it would make another $82,500 in investment income.

ABC Auto Insurance Company makes money by charging sufficient premium to cover the actual losses incurred and leaving a profit for the company. The key to making money for ABC is the expertise in underwriting risk. A 20-year-old single male driving a two-door sports car pays a higher auto insurance premium than a 30-year-old married female driving a minivan. That determination is made by the underwriters at ABC using statistical estimates of the customer and type of vehicle.

So, by now you are probably wondering how an option selling hedge fund works like an insurance company. How is one option trader able to do everything an insurance company does to make money? Keep on reading. We will show you how to trade options exactly like running an insurance company. A side-by-side comparison of the automobile insurance to writing (or selling) a put is shown in Table 1.1.

Table 1.1 shows a side-by-side comparison of auto insurance and option selling. Remember that options are a form of financial insurance. They transfer risks from the option buyer to the option seller. Auto insurance is just like options:

1. First, there is an asset being insured. In the case of auto insurance, the asset insured is the car. In options the asset being insured is the stock, index, or future.

2. Every insurance contract is in effect for a specific time period. In auto insurance the policy usually is for 12 months. In options the period varies depending on the options you buy or sell, and it could range from a duration of one week to 30 months. In this example the option expires in 30 days.

3. For auto insurance there is an amount that is insured, the value of the vehicle. In this example it is a $20,000 car. In options the strike price defines the amount insured. In this case it's $90; this means that the owner of the put has the right to sell XYZ stock at $90 before the option expires. This is like auto insurance: If the vehicle is worth $20,000 and gets into an accident that causes $4,500 in damages, then the auto insurance company needs to make the policy holder whole and pay for the repairs needed to bring back the value of the vehicle to $20,000.

Table 1.1 Auto Insurance Comparisons to Option Selling

	Auto Insurance Terminology		Option Selling Terminology	
1	Insured asset	Car	Underlying asset	XYZ stock (trading at $100)
2	Insured period	12 months	Time to option expiration	30 days
3	Value insured	$20,000	Strike price	$90
4	Deductible	$2,000 (10% of insured value)	% OTM (out-of-the-money)	10% (XYZ was trading at $100 when $90 put was sold)
5	Insurance premiums	$1,000	Option premiums	$3
6	Loss ratio	10%	Probability of profit	90%
7	Claims	Yes: Pay out claim No: Keep premium	Expired	ITM[1]: Seller has to buy XYZ for $90 OTM[2]: Option seller keeps the premium
8	Reinsurance	Buy insurance from another company to protect against catastrophic loss (e.g., a tsunami)	Hedge	Buy XYZ put farther OTM or index puts to protect against large market losses (e.g., 9/11/01 attacks)

[1] ITM: In-the-money option is an option that has intrinsic value.

[2] OTM: Out-of-the-money option is an option that has no intrinsic value.

4. To pay less for auto insurance, some car owners are willing to take some risk by agreeing to a deductible in the car insurance contract. In this example, the car owner is willing to pay for the first $2,000 of damages in a claim. Hence, if the car gets in an accident and the repairs are $4,500, the insured will have to pay $2,000 and will be reimbursed $2,500 from the insurance company. This is analogous to selling OTM (out-of-the-money) puts. The option buyer, to pay less for the put that's protecting XYZ stock, is willing to assume 10% of the loss if XYZ stock goes down. So, instead of buying a put with a $100 strike price, he buys a put with a $90 strike price. That means that if XYZ stock's price falls within $0 to $10, or up to 10%, then the owner of the put will not get anything back from the put if held to expiration. He is willing to absorb the first 10% of the fall in XYZ.

5. A premium is paid for insurance, the same as for options. In both auto insurance and options the fee paid for the contract is called a premium. In the example, the car owner paid $1,000 to insure the car for 12 months. The option buyer paid $3 to insure 100 stocks of XYZ at a price of $90 for 30 days.

6. From the ABC Auto Insurance Co. point of view, there is a loss ratio based on actuarial tables expected from selling the auto insurance. In this example ABC expects to have a 10% loss ratio. This means that on average from the auto insurance segment, it expects to have claims on 10% of its policies. From the option seller perspective when writing the put, according to the analytical model used, the XYZ put has a 90% probability of expiring worthless. The underwriting is very important when one is running an insurance business. This topic is addressed in a later chapter.

7. In auto insurance either the company pays out a claim when there is a loss, or it does not have to pay out anything if the policy holder is claims free. In the latter case, the insurance company would have made money since it keeps the entire premium. It is the same case for the option seller. If the put option sold expires in-the-money (ITM), the option seller will have to buy XYZ stock

for $90 from the put option owner. If the put expires out-of-the-money (OTM), meaning that XYZ was above $90 at the time of expiration, then the put seller keeps the premium collected.

8. Most insurance companies reinsure part of their risk. For example, ABC Insurance Company might buy earthquake and tsunami insurance from a reinsurance company to cover all the automobiles for which ABC has written insurance. This is done to avoid a catastrophic event. If there were a tsunami, most likely there would be closer to 100% loss instead of 10% expected loss. Hence, reinsurance against catastrophic losses is a good idea. The option seller can do the same to protect against a catastrophic event (e.g., 9/11/2001, a financial meltdown, or a presidential assassination) by buying a put at lower strikes (OTM) in XYZ or by buying an OTM put at the market (S&P 500 index). By doing this, the options seller reinsures just like the insurance companies to avoid catastrophic losses.

The example shows that selling options is very much like running an insurance company. The business of a one-man insurance company is to collect premiums from option buyers in exchange for the risks of losses in the underlying markets of the options and earn profits from the time decay of the options.

How Insurance Companies Lose Money

Understanding the business is crucial to your success. Now that you know how insurance companies make money, let's talk about how they lose money. The insurance business is fabulous; just make sure you know what you are getting into. Make sure you understand the risks.

Insurance companies can lose money in their investments or on the insurance contracts they have written. Losses from investments are losses that the company had with the float (its reserves). The losses from insurance contracts, commonly known as underwriting losses, come from insurance contracts on which the company had to pay claims. When the claims are more than the premiums received, there is an underwriting loss. The insurance company lost money because it mispriced the insurance by underestimating the risk. This is why knowing the risk is extremely important in order to not lose money in this business.

The most important function in the insurance company is underwriting. Underwriters select and price risk. They make sure that actuarially the policies written are expected to have a positive return. For example, in a life insurance policy, the underwriting unit is the one that figures out how long a 40-year-old male, nonsmoker, with a clean bill of health is expected to live. Then with this information they figure out how much to price the premium for the life insurance for this segment of the population in order to have a positive expected return.

If the underwriting unit is wrong, the loss ratio will be higher than expected, and the company will lose money. They will pay out more than they collect in premiums.

This sounds like a simple business, but it is not. The company estimates the probability of losses to a segment it wants to insure. Next, based on those estimates, it prices the premium needed to make a profit. Then, it sells the insurance policies. It collects the premiums and invests them while it waits for the policy to expire or the event to happen. Finally, if the event happens it pays out the claim, or if the event does not happen it pockets the premiums as profits.

Where is the ugly, you ask? Overall, insurance is a good business. However, the ugly comes when there are risks that are hard to calculate. The financial crisis of 2008, when AIG almost went under and the U.S. Government bailed it out, is an example of the ugly. AIG was selling credit insurance, credit default swaps (CDS), to insure mortgage-backed securities. However, it did not calculate the risks correctly, and when subprime mortgages started blowing up, AIG was in big trouble. AIG sold $450 billion of credit insurance without a clear understanding of how the risks behaved. When the subprime mortgages started to default, the underlying mortgage-backed bonds insured by AIG started failing and AIG was caught without enough liquidity to back the securities it had sold. It turned ugly very fast and was due to poor underwriting. AIG did not know the risks it took on and did not collect the necessary premiums to cover the risks. In fact, it didn't manage its portfolio of risks correctly because it was overexposed to subprime mortgage risks without knowing their magnitude. It was a disaster that almost brought down the entire financial system. That's the ugly.

Insurance companies sell "paper," a promise to pay in the future in exchange for cash now. In the future who knows whether it will have to pay or not, but most likely it will pay out less than the cash it collected.

Success Drivers of the Insurance Business

The key for an insurance company to be successful boils down to doing four things right:

1. Risk Selection: Identifying the risk it is willing to take, which means being good at underwriting and pricing.

2. Risk Management: Managing risk, reinsuring unwanted risk, and managing claims effectively.

3. Risk Acquisition: Subscribing insurance, using sales channels, and effective marketing to attract clients and sell insurance policies.

4. Investment Operations: Earning good returns on the reserves (or float).

Reviewing the value chain, Figure 1.2, as you compare the traditional insurance company value chain to TOMIC's simplified value chain, you see that their functions and their success factors are the same. The investment operations of TOMIC are very simple. TOMIC keeps the required reserves in money market funds or in cash.

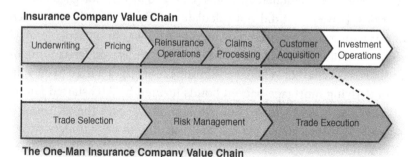

Insurance Company Value Chain

| Underwriting | Pricing | Reinsurance Operations | Claims Processing | Customer Acquisition | Investment Operations |

| Trade Selection | Risk Management | Trade Execution |

The One-Man Insurance Company Value Chain

Figure 1.2 Comparison between value chains of a traditional insurance company and TOMIC.

TOMIC's value chain has three primary functions:

1. Trade Selection: Encompasses underwriting and pricing. Selects the market and strategies to trade.

2. Risk Management: Encompasses money management, trade sizing, hedging (reinsurance), trade adjustment (claims), and trade decisions.

3. Trade Execution: Is the equivalent of client acquisition in the traditional insurance company. In this case TOMIC goes to the option exchanges to sell its options (insurance policies).

These success drivers need to be managed in any insurance company that wants profits. At The One Man Insurance Company you need to constantly watch and manage these drivers to avoid ugly results:

1. Trade selection. This function encompasses selecting markets, pricing the risk, and selecting a strategy and a timeframe. Allstate and State Farm select geographic regions where they sell homeowners insurance. It is the same process in The One Man Insurance Company (TOMIC), but instead of homes in different geographies, TOMIC selects which underlying indexes or equities markets it will write options on. TOMIC could write options on the SPX, RUT, NDX, DIA, AAPL, IBM, PG, JNJ, or GOOG, to name a few. Pricing of the insurance is very important. In an insurance company like Allstate the underwriting department defines the expected losses for a specific group of insured. For example, for automobile insurance they would use variables to predict expected losses from a segment of drivers. They know to expect fewer crashes from married women age 32, driving a minivan, than for single males age 18, driving a two-seat convertible. At TOMIC the pricing is very similar. The difference is that you are the underwriter and will need to know the volatility and price of the underlying equity or index you are going to insure (write options against). Once you know the market and the risk you want to take, you select a strategy. Your strategy selection could be a vertical spread, calendar spread, condor, and so on. Finally, you should decide on a timeframe for the trade—a week, 20 days, 30 days, and so on. Homes are usually insured on an annual basis.

2. Risk management. This function could be more accurately called active risk management. This function continuously monitors the risk portfolio and divests any risk that is not wanted. At Allstate if the loss ratio on married women driving minivans starts increasing year after year, they have to determine what has changed. Maybe it is that the women have more children who cause distractions when the women are driving. Given that they are constantly monitoring their insurance portfolio, Allstate adjusts (raises) the price of the insurance for this market, or they might not insure married women with kids driving minivans. The same should happen at TOMIC. For example, if TOMIC insures defense contractors and new legislation from Congress cuts defense spending by half, TOMIC might stop writing options on defense contractors or it might reinsure its position by buying puts. TOMIC has to constantly be aware of changes in volatilities and prices of the underlying market. Risk management at TOMIC involves position sizing, money management, trade adjustments, portfolio insurance, and portfolio diversification.

3. Trade Execution. This function is equivalent to the sales of insurance policies by the traditional insurance sales force. Instead of having agents like Allstate, at TOMIC we have the option exchanges. TOMIC goes to an option exchange, using a broker, to buy or sell options. There is no need for a sales force to sell insurance, only a computer connected to an exchange. The efficiency and effectiveness in which TOMIC can execute a trade will have a direct impact on profitability. There are different ways to execute a complex trade, and there are many factors that impact the execution. The factors could be the size of the market, size of the trade, the time of day, the exchanges the market is traded on, and the market makers. This function is a crucial link to having a successful TOMIC or not, and you must know how to execute your trades well.

All the key success factors of an insurance business need to be in place at TOMIC in order to have an ongoing successful business. TOMIC operating profitably and successfully is, in theory, achievable. Figure 1.3 shows what TOMIC looks like when you include all of its functions: primary and support.

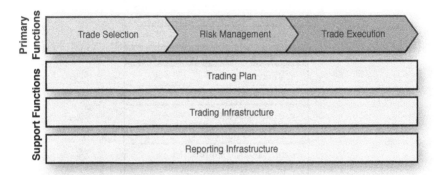

Figure 1.3 TOMIC value chain.

Every business has some kind of "infrastructure" before it begins to operate. For example, a fast-food franchise needs real estate, stoves, refrigerators, and telephones. At TOMIC, you need hardware (computers, Internet connections, and telephones), software (trading software and a plan), and working capital in order to operate. For TOMIC to execute its functions (trade selection, risk management, and trade execution), it needs to have a set of supporting functions in place. The supporting functions allow you to operate TOMIC successfully. These functions are divided into trading plan, trading infrastructures, and learning processes. Table 1.2 shows an outline of the supporting functions and their important processes.

Table 1.2   TOMIC Supporting Functions

Trading Plan
a. Trade goals
b. Markets to trade
c. Strategy selection parameters
d. Risk management checklist
e. Entry/exit plans
f. Checklists
Trading Infrastructure
a. Broker
b. Execution software
c. Analysis software
d. Portfolio margin
e. Information sources
f. Risk capital
Learning Processes
a. Trading journal
b. Trading group
c. Trading coach
d. Continuing education plan

The trading plan is the operational plan of a traditional insurance company. The trading plan specifies trade goals, the markets to trade, the strategies, the risk management parameters, and the entries and exits. The trading plan is the operational guideline for the manager of TOMIC. It describes the parameters in which TOMIC should operate.

The trading infrastructure is the collection of brokers, execution software, analysis software, information resources, portfolio margin, and risk capital.

The learning processes are a set of habits TOMIC needs in order to continuously improve its business. This function contains a trading journal, a trading group, a trading coach, and a continuing education plan.

In this chapter, we provided you with an overview of the insurance business, and we showed you how TOMIC is just like a traditional insurance company. In the subsequent chapters of Part I, we discuss in detail each of the primary functions and support functions of TOMIC's value chain.

2

Trade Selection

rade selection at a hedge fund is the equivalent of the underwriting function in an insurance company. If underwriting is executed correctly and the risk is priced fairly, the business is sound. The business should make money because premiums collected are adequate compensation for the risk taken. If underwriting is executed poorly and the risk being taken is not well defined, the premiums collected might not be enough to cover the risks.

A good example of this is the contrast of two big events. One event is losses from Hurricane Katrina in 2005, and the second is losses on mortgage-backed securities that led to the implosion of AIG in 2008. Both events were big hits to the insurance industry. The first event, Hurricane Katrina, caused a lot of damages and claims. However, the insurance companies were able to survive and profit even with claims resulting from the event.

In a report to Congress in 2008, Rawle King analyzed the insurance losses incurred due to Hurricane Katrina and concluded that the insurers were able to absorb the losses without any problem:

> Catastrophe-insured losses in 2005 totaled $66.1 billion from 24 disasters. Estimated insured losses from Katrina alone were $43.6 billion stemming from 1.75 million claims. Despite the severity of storm damages, Hurricane Katrina and other catastrophes in 2005 did not threaten the solvency and claims-paying ability of the property/casualty (p/c) insurance industry. Insurers benefited from favorable market conditions during the last three years and experienced significant growth in policyholder

surplus. Insurers, in fact, earned record profits in each of the last three years—2004-2006.[1]

The insurance companies were able to profit from Katrina because of sound underwriting. They had previous experiences (Hurricane Andrew, for example) that helped them determine their risk and enabled them to collect the correct amount of premiums.

The second event, AIG's selling of $450 billion of coverage in credit default swaps, was not well underwritten. AIG did not have a clear understanding of how the risks behaved. Pricing insurance for the bonds was not like pricing fire insurance for houses. Pricing CDS (credit default swaps) is very different from pricing fire insurance. If a house in a neighborhood burns down, it doesn't increase the risk of a house in another neighborhood ten miles away burning down. In the CDS market, if a mortgage-backed security failed due to weakening economic conditions, for example an increase in unemployment, other mortgage-backed securities could also fail. AIG did very poor underwriting and it paid its dues in 2008 when the government had to bail it out. It did not understand the risks it was taking on, it didn't price it correctly, and it didn't manage its portfolio correctly. It almost went under.

Hence, trade selection, like insurance underwriting, is the key to this business. TOMIC is built by having a portfolio of risks taken in exchange for premiums collected. TOMIC must know the risks it is taking on. TOMIC cannot insure what it doesn't know. This is where trade selection comes into play. It is probably the most important function at TOMIC, underwriting and the decision-making process on the risks to be acquired. There are several decisions to be made when you're selecting a trade. First, you have to select which markets to trade. Second, you need to find the best available strategy to use for that market. Third, you have to set the duration of the trade. Fourth, you have to know the impact of volatility in your trade. Finally, you will have to decide the price at which you are willing to enter the trade.

Market Selection

The selection of markets (underwriting) is very important. Each market is unique; the markets behave differently. For example, GLD (SPDR

Gold Trust) is a proxy for gold and it behaves much differently than SPY (SPDR S&P 500 ETF), the exchange-traded fund (ETF) that replicates the S&P 500. The difficulty level of trading options on a market depends on your familiarity with that market. For example, GEICO specializes in auto insurance while AFLAC specializes in disability and workers' compensation insurance. Both are insurance companies but they are in different markets. You, as the operator of TOMIC, will have to define the markets you want to play.

You could be a specialist like AFLAC and invest in one or two markets, or you could be like State Farm or Allstate and manage multiple and different markets.

At TOMIC the markets are broken down into four classes:

1. Indexes: SPX, NDX, RUT, OEX.

2. Exchange-traded funds: SPY, QQQ, IWM, OIH, RTH, XLF, XLE.

3. Equities: AAPL, IBM, MCD, WMT, GS, FCX.

4. Futures: These are not covered in this book; however, they can be traded through diversified commodities indexes or ETCs, exchange-traded commodities.

Indexes

Trading options of indexes provide tax advantages to U.S. citizens. Section 1256 of the Internal Revenue Code addresses how broad-based equity index options are treated. Basically, any gain on the sale of these index options is treated as 60% long-term *capital gain* income and 40% short-term capital gain income. This remains true regardless of the length of time you hold the index option. It also applies whether you are "long" or "short" these index options.

IRC Section 1256 provides a discount because the maximum blended tax rate of an index option is 23% (assuming 35% ordinary gains and 15% long-term capital gains). This rate of 23% is a significant discount against the 35% of ordinary gains you pay if you are in the top bracket. Be aware, though, that the Internal Revenue code is constantly changing, so you and your tax advisor have to make sure these rules still apply.

The indexes we suggest using are SPX, NDX, RUT, DJX, and OEX.

The following list shows the ticker symbols for the different indexes.

Primary Tax Advantaged Index Options

- DJX—Dow Jones Industrial Average
- OEX—S&P 100 Index Options (American style)
- XEO—S&P 100 Index Options (European style)
- SPX—S&P 500 Index Options
- XSP—Mini-S&P 500 Index Options
- NDX—NASDAQ 100 Index Options
- MNX—CBOE Mini-NDX Index Options
- RUT—Russell 2000 Index Options

The following are the benefits of IRC Section 1256. Make sure to consult with your tax advisor.

60-40 Tax Treatment

- Applies to broad-based, cash-settled index options.
- IRS Section 1256 contracts.
- Regardless of holding period, profits are treated as 60% long-term and 40% short-term.
- Reported on Form 6781 and Schedule D.
- Positions are "Marked to Market" at year end and taxed as if closed. Year-end prices become cost basis for the next tax year.

If you decide to trade options on indexes you should make sure that the options have enough liquidity. You can do this by checking the option open interest (see Figure 2.1). The index with the most option interest is the SPX. This market is very liquid and should be on the top of your list.

Exchange-Traded Funds (ETFs)

Exchange-traded funds are very similar to indexes. ETFs consist of a basket of equities that trade like a stock and may also mirror an index. It is best to use liquid ETFs with options trading.

CBOE Index Open Interest on 2/21/2012							
Option	Calls	Puts	Total	Option	Calls	Puts	Total
OEX	28354	33700	62054	OEX post exp	N/A	N/A	N/A
SPX	3840688	6889168	10729856	SPX post exp	N/A	N/A	N/A
NDX	117781	189126	306907	NDX post exp	N/A	N/A	N/A
MNX	58976	89474	148450	MNX post exp	N/A	N/A	N/A
DJX	113225	115326	228551	DJX post exp	N/A	N/A	N/A

Figure 2.1 Chicago Board Options Exchange (CBOE) options open interest. (Source: www.cboe.com/data/IntraDayVol.aspx.)

For a current list of ETFs with options, refer to the Chicago Board Options Exchange (CBOE) Web site www.cboe.com. The following is a sample list of ETF options traded on the CBOE.

DIA—Options on DIAMONDS

DVY—iShares DJ Select Dividend

EEM—iShares MSCI Emerging Markets Index

EWZ—iShares MSCI Brazil Index Fund

FXE—CurrencyShares Euro Trust

FXI—iShares FTSA/Xinhua China 25

GLD—Options on SPDR Gold Shares

IBB—iShares Nasdaq Biotechnology

ILF—iShares S&P Latin America 40 Index

IWM—iShares Russell 2000 Index Fund

IYR—iShares DJ U.S. Real Estate

IYT—iShares Dow Jones U.S. Transportation Average Index Fund

KRE—KBW Regional Banking ETF

MDY—Standard & Poor's MidCap 400 Index

MOO—Market Vectors Global Agribusiness ETF

OIH—Oil Services HOLDRs Trust

QQQ—PowerShares QQQ Trust

RTH—Retail HOLDRs Trust

SPY—SPDR S&P 500 ETF Trust

SLV—iShares Silver Trust

TLT—iShares Lehman 20+ Year Treasury Bond Fund

USO—United States Oil Fund

XBI—SPDR Biotech ETF

XES—SPDR SPDR Oil & Gas Equipment & Services ETF

XHB—SPDR Homebuilders ETF

XLB—Materials Select Sector SPDR

XLE—Energy Select Sector SPDR

XLF—Financial Select Sector SPDR

XLI—Industrial Select Sector SPDR

XLK—Technology Select Sector SPDR

XLP—Consumer Staples Select Sector SPDR

XLU—Utilities Select Sector SPDR

XLV—Health Care Select Sector SPDR

XLY—Consumer Discretionary Select Sector SPDR

XME—SPDR S&P Metals & Mining ETF

XOP—SPDR S&P Oil & Gas Exploration & Production ETF

XRT—SPDR SPDR S&P Retail ETF

You need to ensure that options are liquid (with open interest greater than 500 per strike price); also make sure that there is adequate daily volume in the ETF. Volume data is provided by CBOE or other exchanges.

Options on Equities

Using options on liquid equities is advisable. Liquid equities are those with enough trading volume and with options trading allowed.

Check the CBOE for average daily volume. Table 2.1 shows a sample of the month of April 2011. This table shows the top 50 (sorted by average daily volume) underlying equity options in that month.

Table 2.1   Top 50 Option Markets Sorted by Average Option Daily Volume (Source: www.cboe.com/data/AvgDailyVolArchive.aspx)

Symbol	Opt Sym	Name	Call	Put	Total
C	C	Citigroup, Inc.	1,682,214	673,598	2,355,812
AAPL	AAQ	Apple, Inc.	809,044	638,526	1,447,570
BAC	BAC	Bank of America Corporation	737,488	556,135	1,293,623
CSCO	CYQ	Cisco Systems, Inc.	591,650	332,866	924,516
F	F	Ford Motor Company	544,124	231,556	775,680
INTC	INQ	Intel Corporation	423,569	252,374	675,943
MSFT	MQF	Microsoft Corporation	462,359	191,885	654,244
JPM	JPM	JPMorgan Chase & Co.	273,420	230,059	503,479
NFLX	QNQ	NetFlix, Inc.	223,602	253,335	476,937
GE	GE	General Electric Company	283,956	183,626	467,582
LVS	LVS	Las Vegas Sands Corp.	352,107	105,227	457,334
RIMM	RUL	Research in Motion Limited	233,316	216,974	450,290
BIDU	BDQ	Baidu, Inc. ADS	300,005	147,808	447,813
AMZN	ZQN	Amazon.com, Inc.	231,075	208,601	439,676
GOOG	GOQ	Google, Inc.	244,089	193,746	437,835
AA	AA	ALCOA, Inc.	230,707	196,895	427,602
SLW	SLW	Silver Wheaton Corporation	272,126	131,048	403,174
GM	GM	General Motors Corporation	187,043	143,977	331,020
FCX	FCX	Freeport-McMoRan Copper & Gold Co., Inc. (Class B)	190,225	139,565	329,790

Symbol	Opt Sym	Name	Call	Put	Total
WFC	WFC	Wells Fargo & Company	175,420	145,554	320,974
PFE	PFE	Pfizer, Inc.	205,449	114,842	320,291
YHOO	YHQ	Yahoo! Inc.	207,389	69,830	277,219
XOM	XOM	Exxon Mobil Corporation	148,325	119,419	267,744
POT	POT	Potash Corporation of Saskatchewan, Inc.	154,896	89,659	244,555
GS	GS	The Goldman Sachs Group, Inc.	125,132	115,991	241,123
TIVO	TUK	TiVo, Inc.	164,371	70,354	234,725
X	X	United States Steel Corporation	148,457	72,388	220,845
PBR	PBR	Petroleo Brasileiro S.A.-ADR	135,604	79,054	214,658
IBM	IBM	International Business Machines Corporation	121,423	89,864	211,287
QCOM	QAQ	QUALCOMM, Inc.	134,641	76,304	210,945
T	T	AT&T Corporation	114,003	81,275	195,278
CAT	CAT	Caterpillar, Inc.	98,972	95,378	194,350
BP	BP	BP plc.	130,491	62,164	192,655
VALE	RIO	Vale SA	98,087	87,716	185,803
MU	MU	Micron Technology, Inc.	129,115	55,129	184,244
NOK	NOK	Nokia Corporation ADR	140,959	38,086	179,045
SINA	NOQ	SINA Corporation	123,770	51,875	175,645
AMRN	AMRN	Amarin Corporation	144,473	31,087	175,560
ORCL	ORQ	Oracle Corporation	108,428	64,985	173,413
MGM	MGM	MGM Resorts International	122,650	49,152	171,802
JNJ	JNJ	Johnson & Johnson	98,839	72,821	171,660
NVDA	UVA	NVIDIA Corporation	124,210	46,989	171,199

Symbol	Opt Sym	Name	Call	Put	Total
VLO	VLO	Valero Energy Corp	132,716	38,441	171,157
STX	STX	Seagate Technology	121,553	49,583	171,136
TYC	TYC	Tyco International Limited	139,490	31,168	170,658
MCP	MCP	Molycorp, Inc.	104,242	64,746	168,988
UAL	UAL	United Continental Holdings, Inc.	110,487	53,275	163,762
ABX	ABX	Barrick Gold Corporation	110,999	48,741	159,740
HPQ	HWP	Hewlett-Packard Company	97,626	61,182	158,808

If an underlying equity has options with daily volume greater than 50,000 contracts, you can consider that market liquid.

Select a few equities and follow them closely to learn their behavior. Also, diversify your markets. Select multiple industries or sectors. For example, if you wanted to use five different markets, a diversified selection could be AAPL, JPM, FCX, LVS, and BP.

Strategy Selection

Strategy selection and trade construction are the crux of the business. Your ability to select the strategies and set up trades giving you the best chance of profiting is one of the main factors in a successful TOMIC.

To select your strategy, answer the following:

1. Which market(s) are you going to trade?

2. What is the direction?

3. What is the time frame?

4. What is the volatility of the underlying and its options?

5. What is the risk/reward?

The market you choose impacts your strategy selection. The current price of the underlying and its liquidity influences the number of strikes available to trade and the distance between strikes. Stock priced at $15 does not price out the same as stock priced at $300. For example, in the $15 stock it would be harder to trade vertical spreads than it would be in a $300 stock.

As for the direction of the underlying, there are three possibilities: up, down, or sideways. Having an opinion of the direction that the underlying will move is important in determining the strategy selection you will use. However, it is possible to still make money without being 100% correct in the direction. To obtain an opinion of direction of the underlying, some traders use technical analysis, some use fundamental analysis, and some use a combination of both. Study both and use what is most comfortable for you.

Time Frame

"You win battles by knowing the enemy's timing, and using a timing which the enemy does not expect."

—Miyamoto Musashi, 17th-century Japanese swordsman and rōnin

The trading time frame is another factor in trade selection. For example, when you buy insurance, do you go with a six-month policy or an annual policy? The price varies depending on the time frame you insure, so you pay less per day if you buy an annual policy. As a TOMIC trader, you will decide whether to write a six-month or annual policy. In fact, the time frames used at TOMIC could be weeks, months, quarters, semesters, or years.

You can trade weekly options in many indexes and stocks. For example, the CBOE offers weekly options on the SPX and select equities like AAPL. You may also write monthly options or LEAPS as far away as 30 months.

Your decision on time frame is based on your prediction of behavior of the underlying and the volatility of the options in the different time frames. For example, if you think SPX will go sideways for the next year and volatility across the different months seems to have a stable relationship, then a calendar spread might work well for you. Another choice is a shorter duration trade such as a monthly iron condor or butterfly, depending on volatility.

Volatility

The volatility of the underlying and the options used in the strategy creates another factor. If you operate an insurance company selling hurricane insurance in Florida and in the Cayman Islands, assume you have data revealing that for the past 150 years Florida gets hit by a major hurricane on average every 12 years, and the Cayman Islands gets hit every 2 years. Will you charge the same price for insuring homes of equal value in Florida and in the Cayman Islands? Of course not. You would expect that the Cayman Islands hurricane insurance would cost more. By the same reasoning, volatility impacts the selection of markets and the price of insurance.

Most people ignore this factor in strategy selection. However, knowing volatility will help you in your choices. To figure out which is better between a calendar spread and a butterfly, for example, if you believe the market is going sideways, the deciding factor will be volatility. You use not only the volatility of the underlying, but also the volatility curve of the options (volatility across different strike prices), and the term structure (volatility across different expirations).

The risk/reward factors into your selection. This defines your edge. Your reward goes hand in hand with risk. However, sometimes you get an asymmetric risk/reward function in which your reward pays better for the risk taken. In these scenarios the trade has an edge, which is a very large factor in selecting your trade. This topic is covered in more detail in Chapter 8, "Understanding Volatility."

Pricing

The price of a trade, whether buying or selling, is the final factor in trade selection. Volatility and price go hand in hand. If you compare an option in a high-volatility environment against the same option in a low-volatility environment, the option prices should be directly proportional to volatility. This is the case of the example of a house in Florida and the same house in the Cayman Islands. In theory, under ideal conditions, assuming that all hurricanes cause the same amount of damage, the Cayman hurricane insurance should be priced at six times the price of the Florida insurance.

Prices in insurance are not fixed, just as prices in the options exchanges; it is a market-based system. So if the price of Cayman hurricane insurance is only twice the price of Florida's insurance, something does not add up. One or the other is priced poorly.

Under this scenario, where is your edge? Should you sell Florida insurance or should you sell Cayman insurance? The price impacts your decision, right? The correct thing to do is to sell Cayman insurance and buy Florida insurance.

This hurricane-insurance scenario is the same reasoning process for every trade in TOMIC. Pricing determines whether you do a trade. And pricing is driven by these factors: underlying, strategy, time frame, and volatility.

Putting all this together, you select a trade. You underwrite the risk and decide what to insure and at what price in order to make a profit.

Endnote

1. Rawle King, 1/31/2008, CRS Report to Congress, "Hurricane Katrina: Insurance Losses and National Capacities for Financing Disaster Risks," summary.

3

Risk Management

"Risk. Risk is our business. That's what this starship is all about. That's why we're aboard her."

—James T. Kirk, USS *Enterprise, Star Trek,*
"Return to Tomorrow," Ep. 51/4768.3

Any hedge fund, including TOMIC, is in the business of risk taking. It is not in the business of risk avoidance. According to Will Rogers, "You've got to go out on a limb sometimes because that's where the fruit is."

The business of TOMIC is to subscribe risk. TOMIC makes a living from taking other people's risk in exchange for a premium. Taking risk is what pays the bills at TOMIC. In fact, everything in life carries a certain degree of risk. If people did not perceive risk, they would not buy insurance. If the stock market did not have risk, no one would pay the premiums for the options. We cannot avoid risk, but we can manage it. When you cross a street you are taking a risk. A car could hit you. But you manage the risk by looking both ways before crossing. Even so, a crazy sniper could shoot you from the top of a building when you are crossing the street. If you are living, you are constantly taking risks and you are constantly managing those risks. The trick to making money at TOMIC is managing the risk by being aware of exactly what risk you are willing to take and divesting or reinsuring the risk you do not want to take.

In the preceding chapter on trade selection, you saw how TOMIC identifies the risks it wants to take and at what price. TOMIC has to make sure it receives enough compensation for the risk. TOMIC has to manage the portfolio risk to avoid losses due from unexpected risks. Taking losses from identified risks is acceptable, but getting blindsided from unexpected risks is not.

Risk Management

Risk management is a continuous process involving everything from underwriting (selecting the trade), sizing of positions, and active money management. Risk management should be ingrained in every TOMIC trader's DNA. Risk management should be part of the entire process of managing TOMIC.

To manage the risk of TOMIC, you need to be able to answer all the following questions.

Before the trade:

- What is the risk/reward ratio of this trade?
- What is the probability of success of this trade?
- What is the maximum loss acceptable for this trade?
- What is the expected return and target profit of this trade?
- Does the new trade maintain the balance or diversification of the portfolio? Is it overexposed in any one sector?

During the trade:

- Has the trade reached the maximum allowed loss?
- Has the trade reached the target profit?
- Is the reward of keeping the trade open worth the risk?

After the trade:

- Did you follow the risk management rules on this trade?
- If you did not, why not?

You may have heard successful investors like Warren Buffet say, *"Rule number one is never lose money. Rule number two is never forget rule number one.*" The secret to implementing Buffet's rule number one is to have a disciplined risk management process in place.

To manage its risk, TOMIC needs to do the following:

1. Create a money management policy.

2. Define a position sizing policy.

3. Maintain a diversified portfolio.

4. Adjust the trades or exit when a trade goes bad.

5. Buy portfolio insurance to protect against black swan events.

Money Management

Many traders have blown up their accounts. In some cases they have blown up several accounts and had to stop trading for a time. Some of them have had to give up trading altogether. Money management is a very serious issue. Most people, when they start trading, are so excited that they are quick to open and fund the account. As soon as the account is opened, the first thing they do is place a trade. However, the first thing you should do is make sure you have money management rules in place.

Money management rules are your safety net to help avoid blowing up the account. The worst thing that could happen is losing your capital and being unable to trade anymore. One of Dennis's trading instructors, Dr. Alexander Elder, told him that there are two types of threats everyone should watch out for: sharks and piranhas.

The shark threat is that losing trade that takes out a big chunk of your account. It is a big painful bite that will severely damage your account. It also damages you psychologically. Just imagine wiping out 35% of your equity in one trade. That is a real shark bite.

The piranha threat is what happens when you have a sequence of small losses that overwhelm you. Have you seen the videos of how piranhas kill a cow in the Amazons? They take a lot of small bites and end up eating the cow. Same with your trading account: If you have a lot of small losses, your account will shrink and die.

It is very important that your account prevail against your bad trades, whether piranhas or sharks. Specific money management rules are wise. For example, you can set two primary rules. First, never risk more than 2% of capital on any single trade. Second, if in any single month the account loses more than 6%, stop trading for the rest of the month.

The first rule, never risk more than 2% on any single trade, protects against the shark attack. If you keep your risk to 2% on any one trade, your account will be able to survive even if you have a big loss. Yes, losing 2% is not nice, but it won't kill your account.

The second rule, stop trading when you have lost 6% in a single month, protects against the piranha attack. When you have multiple trades go bad in a row and things are going against you, stop and reassess your trading strategies. Maybe your setups are wrong. Maybe the environment changed and you didn't notice. Maybe you are not making good decisions. The point is that if you are down 6% in a month, stop trading and start fresh the following month. Why 6%? This is an arbitrary percentage. Your percentage could be 5%, 6%, 7%, 10%, or any percentage you can live with. The key is to not let the piranhas kill you. You need to be able to trade another day.

Remember; don't let bad trades kill your account. Make sure you have strict money management rules in place and abide by them. When you do this, you will be a step closer to making money.

Position Sizing

The size of the trades should be structured by following sound money management rules: No one trade can risk more than 2% of the capital, and in any month that you lose 6% the fund goes flat and stops trading for that month.

Assume that a fund has $2 million under management. Following the 2% rule means the fund could risk up to $40,000 on one trade. If you trade a RUT condor with 10-point wing-spreads where condor uses $1,000 of margin (assuming Reg-T), you would think you could do 40 RUT condors. That is 40 × $1,000 = $40,000, which is 2% of $2 million. Actually, this is correct if you assume you will let the condor lose the maximum it can. In practice, we usually use a smaller allowed loss before we pull the trade. For example, in the RUT condor we might have a profit target of 15% of margin and an allowed loss of 20% of margin. So if one condor lost $200 (20% of $1,000), you would exit the trade instead of letting it lose the maximum $1,000. If you only allow the trade to risk $200 if you can risk $40,000 (2% of $2 million) per trade, then you could trade up to 200 RUT condors.

A question that comes up a lot is that if the second rule doesn't allow you to lose more than 6% in a month, do you have only three trades on at any time due to the 2% rule? The answer is no. You can have multiple trades on when following the 2% rule, because not all the trades are likely to go against you at the same time. If they do, you are choosing highly correlated trades, which should not be done. On average, if you have 15 to 20 trades on at a time and assume an 80% success rate, you would have three to four trades go against you in any given month. So hitting a 6% loss in a month is unlikely. If you had four bad trades at 2%, the loss would add up to 8%. However, you have to count the contributions from the winning trades. These would have to make less than 2% to yield a net 6% loss for the month. If you did lose 6%, you should stop and reassess your strategies.

Follow strict position sizing based on your money management parameters. These rules will keep your funds safe and keep the account from blowing up.

Portfolio Diversification

In addition to position sizing, TOMIC needs to maintain a diversified portfolio in order to avoid getting hit by any one sector. Even though each position has a maximum exposure, if all the positions are in correlated markets the position sizing will not safeguard the portfolio. For example, let's say TOMIC position sizing guidelines prescribe a maximum portfolio exposure of 2% per position. However, if all its positions are in integrated oil companies, Exxon-Mobil, Chevron, BP Amoco, Conoco Philips, and Petrobras, the position sizing will not safeguard the portfolio because all positions are heavily correlated.

For position sizing to work, TOMIC must be aware of portfolio diversification. TOMIC should try to include multiple sectors or industries in the portfolio. This will help avoid having too much invested in one sector.

To diversify TOMIC's portfolio, a good idea is to have at least five sectors represented. Also, no one sector should represent more than 25% of the portfolio.

For example, TOMIC could have options positions in five markets, such as SPX, AAPL, GS, FCX, and BP. This mix will create good diversification. In addition, no one position should be risking more than 2% of TOMIC's capital.

Adjusting the Different Trades

While TOMIC has open trades, it has to actively manage risks. If a trade is going against TOMIC, it must reduce the losses caused by a bad trade. There will always be bad trades. No one can win 100% of the time. You can avoid losing only if you don't trade.

Adjusting your trades is part of risk management. After you have entered into a trade, making adjustments will make the difference between losing a lot of money and losing a little. TOMIC makes adjustments to protect its capital and minimize losses. Making adjustments does not help you make more money, but it does help you not lose as much. You make adjustments to a trade when it is going against you, not when it is doing fine. One adjustment that should not be overlooked is closing the trade completely. Taking a loss early is sometimes better than staying in a losing trade.

Some people believe that it does not matter what trade you are in—as long as you are an expert at making adjustments, you will make money. Others believe that selecting the trade and the trade entry is more important than the exit. At TOMIC we believe that trade selection is more important than trade exits; however, making adjustments is also very important. You need to master entries, adjustments, and exits to be successful in this business.

Addressable Risks

In this chapter different solutions to manage risk have included the following:

- Money management
- Position sizing
- Diversification
- Unit insurance
- Adjustments

Every position is impacted by different forces going from a macro level to the micro level. When selecting risk management strategies for a portfolio, you need to be aware of the following risks:

- Systemic risk
- Market risk
- Sector risk
- Company risk

Systemic risk is the risk of a financial system collapse that in turn can bring down the larger economy. An example of systemic risk was the effect of the collapse of Lehman Brothers in 2008 on the rest of the financial market. This collapse started a chain reaction that froze the credit markets in the U.S. and all over the world, and almost brought down the entire financial system. A failure of one company should not bring down an entire system or have such a great impact to the larger economy. However, it did. The world economy came to its knees. It is very difficult to hedge against systemic risk. If the financial systems fail, you might not know whether the paper hedged will hold. For example, the owners of credit default swaps backed by AIG might have lost their protection if AIG had gone under. The way to guard against a systemic failure is to own real assets such as physical gold and silver.

Market risks are macro events impacting the entire market, in which almost all stocks will get hit. Examples of macro events include the 9/11 attacks on the World Trade Center and the 2008 financial crisis in the U.S. These events moved the markets, and it didn't matter which stocks you had. Market risks can be hedged with options. Buy portfolio insurance, for example. Unit puts provide good protection for these kinds of events.

Sector risks are events affecting a specific sector. For example, if the U.S. is cutting defense spending, the defense sector companies will all be hit negatively. Another example: If the U.S. were to impose a new tax on financial institutions, the entire financial sector would be impacted.

Company risks are events specific to the individual company. Examples of these events include the total collapse of Enron and the BP spill in the Gulf Coast. Another example is the death of a key executive like Steve Jobs at Apple. These are events specific to individual companies. The company risks can be hedged easily with options, and by keeping a diversified portfolio.

Risks range from the macro to the micro and there are different ways to mitigate the different levels of risks. Table 3.1 contains examples of risk management solutions for different types of risk.

Table 3.1   Risk Mitigation Examples

Type of Risk	Risk Management Solution
Systemic risk	Holding of real assets like physical gold and silver
Market risk	Unit puts against black swans, VIX calls
Sector risk	Sector diversification, and the use of options
Company risk	Company diversification, and the use of options

Insuring the Portfolio Against Black Swan Events

Insuring or reinsuring unwanted risk is a very important function at TOMIC. TOMIC is not willing to take catastrophic risks. An example of a catastrophic risk is a 25% loss in the market in a single day. TOMIC should manage its risk like a traditional insurance company. For example, a traditional auto insurance company would reinsure the risk it does not want to carry.

Assume that ABC Insurance Co. (a fictitious American property and casualty insurance company) has a lot of cars insured in the San Francisco Bay Area. This region is prone to seismic activity. If San Francisco were to suffer a large earthquake, all the cars that ABC Insurance Co. insured would suffer damages. ABC would have a lot of claims. ABC Insurance Co. wants to insure cars against normal driving scenarios, but not a big earthquake. ABC wouldn't want to take the catastrophic risk of having all their insured vehicles having losses at the same time due to an earthquake. Hence, ABC would reinsure the catastrophic risk with a reinsurance company like General Re (a Berkshire Hathaway subsidiary), thus taking only the risk of the normal daily routines, and giving someone else the earthquake risk.

The divesting of unwanted risks is exactly the same thing that the risk management functions perform at TOMIC. TOMIC is willing to take the risk of normal moves in the market, such as plus or minus 5% price movement, but it reinsures the catastrophic risk beyond. To reinsure this risk, TOMIC could buy out-of-the-money puts on the S&P 500 to protect against a large (25%) downturn in the market. Another alternative to reinsure could be to buy out-of-the-money calls on the VIX. This assumes that a large drop in the S&P 500 would lead to a large spike in the VIX. Depending on the pricing of the SPX puts and the VIX calls, TOMIC could use one or both options to offload the catastrophic risk.

Units Can Save Your Portfolio

The following is an example of how to protect your portfolio against a black swan event. Look back to the flash crash of May 2010. A fund had entered a May OEX butterfly that had been doing reasonably well, until the first week of May. The market began to fall away from the short strikes. At one point the trade was down almost 10% on the butterfly, even after all the hedging and adjusting had been done. Then on May 6, the flash crash happened, and the position made a killing. Why? Because the fund was long what most market makers call "units." These units enabled the butterfly position, which by itself got killed by the crash, to be protected by the options.

A unit is an inexpensive option with unpredictable Greeks. You can break them down relative to product, so that the more expensive the underlying, the more expensive the unit. For instance, in SPY an option becomes a unit around 20 cents; in the SPX an option is a unit closer to

2.00. All units will have deltas below 5 and little to no gamma or vega. So how do these units work?

One of the major issues with most models, especially those used by the retail world, is that they predict uniform increases in volatility. This simply is not the case. When the market makes a violent move downward, two things happen:

1. Front month options increase in value far more than any other month, in relative terms.

2. Downside puts gain far more value than the model predicts.

Think of the volatility curve in a strong down move like a thin piece of wood evenly balanced over a fulcrum. If a fat guy jumps on one side of the wood, what will happen? As with a seesaw, the more you move down the board away from the fulcrum, the more in distance the wood will have moved. There is another factor though: Since the fat guy jumped on the piece of wood, the wood will have moved violently, causing the wood farthest from the fulcrum to temporarily bend upward.

This is the way cheap puts act in a major down move. In the panic, the world is buying ATM puts. Every trader selling or shorting these puts races to buy something to protect the position in case the market tanks.

These shorts buy "units" and all of this buying causes the unit to gain a little price, which increases vega, which increases delta, which increases the value of the unit as the market tanks. This in turn causes the unit to gain more value as traders race to buy these to protect sales, which raises the vega...you get the point—there is a snowball effect.

Here is an example of exactly what happened with the fund in the OEX on April 20. The fund bought the OEX May 505 puts as a hedge against a short iron butterfly. The puts were bought for $1.20. When the market fell on May 6, these options were worth almost $10, and on May 7, they closed at $14.50, a return of over 1,200%. Not bad for an option that cost $1.20.

So how can the ordinary trader use units to increase the returns of his portfolio? Buy units, not a huge amount, but about 5% to 10% of allocated trading money (not the total account value), should go into puts, against a standard set of spread trades (condors, butterflies, and time spreads). This amount should be enough so that, adjusted for any increase in volatility if the market drops 10%, your position no longer loses money and possibly gains. If the market drops 20%, you should be making money.

The math is not that simple. Understanding how units work comes with understanding volatility. By properly implementing units, you are willing to bet that you will never have to sell your house because the market dropped 25%.

4

Trade Execution

Planning needs to be done in sports, in construction, and in trading. In sports or construction, once the game has begun those plans can go out the window. Conditions on the field can change or real estate conditions can affect the development of a skyscraper. The same can hold true in implementing a TOMIC trading plan. However, unlike with sports and construction projects, the TOMIC trader has a much greater ability to control outcomes. The key, as it is in many businesses, is executing a plan in a way that is disciplined but adaptive, a form of having guidelines and an approach without having "trading rules." Just as in a James Dean movie, rules are made to be broken, so traders need to be flexible. In this section you will walk through the process of implementing a TOMIC plan from start to finish. To do so, you will follow a checklist that demands a thought process, guiding you in your trading decisions. Then you will walk through getting an order filled effectively.

Conditions of the Market

The first step is to evaluate the market. At any given time the market can be either volatile or calm. It can have inflated or undervalued implied volatility. Different contract months can be underpriced or overpriced. Within a contract month different strikes can be overpriced or underpriced. With all of these moving parts going back and forth at any given time, the market is going to be more or less favorable to specific trades. Many books and courses teach trading based on entering the same trade every month regardless of conditions; this is an extremely flawed approach. Instead, take the same approach an insurance company would take: See what condition the market is in, and sell an insurance policy that is least likely to be exercised by the buyer. To do so, you need to first understand how to evaluate the situations.

Evaluate Potential Realized Volatility

When Mark was a trader on the floor, one of the things he quickly realized was that he did not need to have an opinion on a company's earnings or an FDA decision, but he did need to know that the event was coming up. TOMIC traders need to have the same approach, especially for nondirectional policy selling. Does the company have earnings, is the federal government releasing important data this week, is the federal reserve having a policy meeting, or is there potential trouble in a far-off place that could potentially affect financial markets? These are all questions you need to be able to answer before moving on. It is somewhat difficult to evaluate the premium in a particular insurance policy without knowing what factors could cause that policy to be enacted.

All the research in the world will not predict earthquakes, terrorist bombings, and other catastrophic events. Reason number one is that looking at HV (historical volatility) can equate to "pissing in the wind." This is why you need to evaluate and have your worst-case scenario in the back of your head at any given time. Looking into the past gives you insight into how the market might react.

If you assume volatility is mean reverting (an assumption the entire option universe relies on), a stock or index moving at an extremely high rate of speed is likely to slow down. A stock moving much more slowly than normal is likely to increase in velocity. Taking this into consideration helps you evaluate how expensive or cheap an insurance policy might be.

Evaluate Implied Volatility

The price of an insurance policy is constantly in flux. At any given time the insurance policy might be expensive or inexpensive. If you assume that HV is mean reverting and this is the basis of IV (implied volatility), you can almost be certain that implied volatility mean will revert as well. This is an important assumption for any trader selling insurance. But is there a way to prove that IV reverts? Rather than run a bunch of numbers, a more interesting way to see proof of expectation of implied volatility mean reversion can be accomplished by looking at VIX options.

The VIX options are cash settled and European-style. Because there is no risk of early assignment, if IV gets too low or too high, the VIX options should not price to the cash market, but toward some expectation of the VIX reverting to its mean. Thus, on an IV spike, in-the-money calls should appear underpriced, and when the VIX is oversold, calls should appear overpriced.

During the flash crash, at 3:30 EST there was still a lot of confusion. The VIX was trading at just under 40%. Take a look at the price differential between the VIX 30 calls and the VIX 47.5 calls, as shown in Figure 4.1.

50.0 calls	MktPr
47.5 calls	1.05
45.0 calls	1.25
42.5 calls	1.55
40.0 calls>	1.90
37.5 calls	2.35
35.0 calls	2.75
32.5 calls	3.30
30.0 calls	3.90

Figure 4.1 Notice the relative price of the 47.5 calls to the 30 calls. (Source: OptionVue6)

Despite one being in-the-money and one out-of-the-money, the two were not that far apart in price. This is because the VIX future was actually trading 29.20, so both were technically out-of-the-money if you look at the futures (although you would consider the 30s the ATM option). Even with the market exploding, the expectations of calming down stopped VIX futures (and thus VIX options) from hitting the 40% that the VIX cash was trading at the time. One interesting thing to note is that the 30s were out-of-the-money in relation to the futures. The relative value of this future compared to the 47.5 calls was quite clear. One of the worst trades in the world is to buy VIX OTM calls in the middle of a crash. The mean reversion of VIX will kill most of these trades.

You will find market expectations of mean reversion, and you can see how to use this assumption in selling insurance. In general, when implied volatility is trading at a premium to its mean, it is likely to be a better sell than a buy. The trader is selling a policy that historically is overpriced. However, this equation is not that simple. There can be good reasons that IV is elevated. This is why you need to walk through step one before evaluating implied volatility. If there is a good reason for IV to be higher, the sale may not be nearly as good as it appears. For a policy to be sold, you need to have a clear picture of the risks of the policy when trading. Only then can you decide that a policy is overpriced.

Evaluate the Months

Once you have an overview of volatility, it is time to get your hands dirty and dig into the nitty-gritty. Evaluating overall volatility is not enough. For an effective TOMIC, you need to evaluate the overall surface, starting with term structure. This is how the different months within a product are priced against one another. Contract months are tightly correlated to each other; however, that does not mean they are tied at the hip. At any given time, paper flow, the direction and size of customers buying or selling options, can cause one month to be more or less expensive than another. By evaluating how the different contract months are priced, you can spot the best month to buy or sell at any given time. It can also present different chances to spread one month against another.

Remember, your goal is to sell the most expensive policy relative to the risk. Finding the most expensive contract month greatly improves collected premiums. There can be different drivers in different months. If you are selling a specific month, or spreading one month against another, doing a little bit of digging to see why the months are priced might reveal a trade that is not nearly as good as it first appears. However, sometimes a large trader with an ax to grind (a major position to put on or take off) can pull the contract months out of whack. When this happens, you should use this information to your advantage.

Evaluate the Skew

One of the most underused and commonly mispriced parts of options is the skew curve. Skew is a term for how cheap or expensive calls and puts are relative to ATM options in reaction to hedging activities. For instance, in equities, IRAs, 401(k)'s, and pension funds, everyone wants to protect against the underlying falling. To do this, most funds employing options collar their positions. This means they buy puts with strikes below current market price and sell calls with strikes above, to help finance the put. This creates puts that are more expensive than ATM options and calls that are less expensive than ATM options. This is not always the case, but if you take a look at the structure of SPX, you can see how hedging activities affect the volatility surface.

Hedging activities are not constant, and at any given time calls and puts can become overpriced or underpriced. The curve moves up or down constantly. Depending on the steepness of the curve, different trades can become more or less favorable as you buy and sell relatively cheap or relatively expensive options. Knowing how expensive the curve is can be a powerful weapon in your arsenal. It helps you determine what trade to enter and where to execute.

Evaluate Other Products

Most SPX trading firms also trade OEX, RUT, NDX, ES, and many individual option names because of the correlation between all the indexes. Traders must be certain not to "fall in love with" one product. For example, the OEX has a beta relative to the SPX of about .98 historically. Yet because of liquidity there are times when they may be significantly overpriced or underpriced relative to the SPX. If you trade one product, you may be missing out on significantly better opportunities in another closely related one. Before entering any trade, figure out whether that is the absolute best trade available at that time. If you like a particular product, you may take the time to explore highly correlated products and walk through the process we just walked through in evaluating those products. Remember, an insurance company does not care who it insures, only that it is selling statistically the best product at the highest price, with the most return.

Trade

Now that you have narrowed your decision to a specific product, it is time to design the trade, then get it executed. To get the best trade, you need to pick strikes, and get the trade filled, as inexpensively as possible.

Picking Strikes

As a large customer buys or sells different strikes up and down the skew curve, specific strikes can become overpriced or underpriced relative to each other. Consistently buying the relatively cheap strike against selling a relatively expensive strike can produce a higher relative credit on credit spreads. Although it might seem small at first, even squeezing out a few pennies per trade can make a big difference in a portfolio. A fully funded TOMIC can trade as many as 15 to 30 trades in and out with more than 1,000 contracts per trade in a given month. That amounts to between 10,000 and 100,000 contracts per month. Improving the average fill price by as little as one cent per contract can add up to big dollars pretty quickly.

The key is to not be married to delta or percentage out-of-the-money. If you want to sell a 10 delta put or call, but the 11 or 9 delta option is the best sale, you are better off selling that option. If you like to sell spreads 5 points wide, but in relative terms the best credit is available by selling 10 or 15 points wide, you should do so. Evaluate the surface when setting up a trade and sell the most expensive option around the strike you studied.

Price

One thing new traders tend to forget is that volatility equates to price. With every cent you give to the market makers, you are selling a slightly lower IV. If you know the IV you are trying to sell, you need to know the equivalent price. Then attempt to execute at that given price. If you cannot get the trade done at your price, you are better off not selling than conceding too much on the trade. Remember, there is an advantage only if you receive the right price.

You might not be able to get a fill at the midprice, but you might not have to. If you know the lowest implied volatility level you are willing to sell down to, you can easily calculate your minimum sale price. To determine how much you are willing to concede, use IV and vega.

For example, suppose the sell side of an option spread has an IV of 21%. This produces a price of $2.00; you are willing to sell the spread down to an IV of 20%. The net vega of the spread is .05. Multiplying .05 × 1% (× 100) produces .05 of flexibility in the spread price. Thus, you are willing to sell the spread down to $1.95, but not any lower.

Order Entry

When Mark was a trader on the floor, he used instant messaging to talk to brokers all the time. Some of the largest institutions in the world would show him some of their "flow," and sometimes he would trade it. That was his job, to make markets and take the other sides of trades. However, there were times when he became the broker. It was then that he had to choose a broker to represent my order. At first he tested every type of broker: floor execution broker, upstairs broker—heck, he even tried representing himself in a crowd or two to get an order filled. Over time he began to learn which brokers could get the best fills for different stocks and ETFs. The number of brokers quickly fell off to very few and eventually he used only three. Why? Because, as with traders, the cream of the brokers rises to the top. He found the best brokers for the specific things he was trying to accomplish and used no one else. They rewarded his loyalty and consistent flow with better fills and lower rates. He never used only one. It was important to him to have the flexibility to send an order to the broker he thought was most likely to give me the best fill.

You might not talk to brokers every day, but you will use a broker every day if you are executing a TOMIC. Selection of the best broker matters for several reasons:

- One broker is going to be better at trading different types of products. If you add futures options to TOMIC, it may become necessary to add a second broker. Most brokers offer everything, but that doesn't make them good at everything. Once your TOMIC is big enough to have money to trade in futures, it should be allocated to the best futures broker. Have money to trade options allocated with the options broker.

- If you are interested in learning or trading a product and the broker doesn't carry the product, consider opening a small account with another firm to learn the product.

- One broker might have better analytics, while lacking great execution. It might become necessary to leave a few dollars with one broker or another just to get real-time data and great analytics.

When selecting an options broker at TOMIC, you should keep a few things in mind.

- Low commissions: When first learning, a low or nonexistent ticket charge is very helpful. However, a ticket charge with lower per-contract commissions typically ends up being a better deal over time.

- The ability to read spread books: One of the things many traders do not realize is how valuable order information can be. When looking through a spread book you can find valuable information such as better offers than the order you are trying to fill, and counter offers to your orders.

- The ability to route orders to an exchange: You need to know that "smart routers" are in fact smart, just not in the way they are presented to the general public. Orders are routed via an algorithm that calculates where the broker will make the most money from the order, not based on where the order is mostly likely to receive the best fill. With the ability to route to specific exchanges, you take away the ability of the algorithm to stop from getting a great fill. Although it may sound trivial, routing to a specific exchange can get trades filled at better prices relative to the price of the underlying. In other words, when buying a call, you will be able to get filled with the stock price slightly higher. It only takes seeing your price trade once on an away exchange while your order doesn't fill to learn this lesson.

Once you have picked the best broker for the product you want to trade, you should pick the best exchange. First route the trade to the exchange with the best bid or offer. The exchange that has the best market will generally provide the best fill, unless the best offer is one of the so-called "maker taker model" exchanges. Interestingly, those exchanges with the best offer will have little effect on your ability to get the order filled.

If the counter bids or offers are all the same, the biggest bids or offers will probably improve things. This belief is unfounded; however, if there is one exchange in particular that trades much larger sizes relative to other exchanges, it may be beneficial to route to that exchange.

The key is to route to exchanges providing the best fills. The best fills occur at two exchanges, the CBOE and the ISE. Next on the list are the PHLX, NYSE-ARCA, and AMEX. These exchanges may be the best to route to if they are particularly dominant in a product. Never route a "maker taker exchange" unless you are hitting a bid or lifting an offer. Market makers almost unilaterally hate paying to fill orders they are hitting, affecting the fill price significantly.

Now that you know what to trade, the next step is how to send in the order. Here are a few ways to get your orders filled.

The first thing you need to know is how small orders are filled. Back in the days before computers, if a complex order came into the crowd, the market makers would price each leg individually, add and subtract the buys and sells, and come up with a market. In that environment, where the market maker could look at the order before it was traded, market makers were willing to improve the price on individual spreads. Spreads offered more security because it was buying one option and selling another, meaning part of the position was already hedged and the trader likely had to sell less underlying to hedge the position entered. Even then if an order got too complex, market makers never liked trades with multiple strikes, different months, weird spreads between strikes, or anything else that was unusual.

Nowadays, things are very different. Complex orders are mostly executed by an algorithm instead of being quoted by the individual trader. Because of this, market makers have to be especially careful of how much edge they are willing to give on any type of order. Firms like Timber Hill and Citadel, much like computer hackers, are constantly testing the exchanges to find weaknesses in the system. If they can pick off a quoting algorithm they will do it quickly, efficiently, and in as much size as they possibly can.

Because of this, the simpler the trade, the more easily you are likely to get it filled. Individual option orders will fill at, relative to the underlying price, better prices than spreads almost all the time. The problem is that this brings the concept of directional risk into the equation for the TOMIC trader, something you are constantly trying to avoid. So buying or selling individual options to set up a spread is not advisable unless you are planning to trade the underlying back and forth as you fill the spread.

In fact, even though the order is going to be tougher to execute, newer traders should almost exclusively put the delta-neutral trade in at once. As you become more experienced at order execution, you should begin to break orders apart. In fact, as a retail trader you will find that you have at one time or another mispriced and could have gotten better fill than breaking the trade up. Remember, individual option quotes are the most efficiently priced; thus, you are less likely to get messed over by market makers, but you may also be less likely to get a great price from the marketplace.

As you become more experienced, first try to fill the whole order. If this cannot be done at an efficient price, break up the trade. This may be your best choice. Call and put spreads are much easier to fill than iron condors or butterflies. In order of difficulty to fill, you can see the best order for breaking apart your trade:

> Nontraditional spreads
>
> Iron condors
>
> Double diagonals
>
> Straddles
>
> Strangles
>
> Butterflies
>
> Vertical spreads
>
> Calendar spreads
>
> Single option trades

One caveat: There are times when a small trade with unusual strikes may fall into a spot in which an algorithm wants to execute the trade. So nontraditional spreads may fill at prices that surprise you.

Size of Order

Trades under ten contracts will have an easier time filling than trades larger than ten. Most algorithms are designed to let the market maker know that there is an order to trade and not set to trade a massive spread, unless it has a ton of edge, or the firm runs an airtight quoting system. Starting small with a spread of fewer than ten contracts helps you get a better fill.

Working an Order

Just because the quote gives a "midprice" does not mean the quote is the midprice. "Book orders" can throw off the bid-ask spread. Book orders can also throw off volatility calculations because they can artificially lower or increase the IV of the calculated midprice. What you are using as a calculation when trading volatility affects this. Once you have established the midpoint, it never hurts to try to do better than that price.

Just because it is a computer quoting the price doesn't mean that it can't screw up. If you have dumped in the wrong IV, the computer might fill the order. Also, a trader or trading group might trade in a manner that causes the trading group to fill the order even if it is above the quoted midprice. Chalk this one up to the "it never hurts to try" category.

Most market makers train for at least a year before "getting on a badge." As a TOMIC trader, you are self-backed, trading your own money. Be as rigid as possible with how you trade and become skilled in getting the absolutely best possible price you can. Remember, saving .05 on a ten-contract trade every day equates to $12,500 a year.

So, to make things easy, here is the thought process I go through and encourage all traders to go through when they enter the market. By following this checklist, traders can develop an approach that will hopefully hone them in on a trade with edge.

Trade Execution Checklist

Before the trade:

- What market are you going to trade?

- What is the direction of the market?

- Did you check the volatility conditions of the market? What is the historical volatility of the market? What is the implied volatility? Did you check the skew?

- What is the strategy you will be using?

- If this is a complex spread, how will it be executed? Is it worth executing at the individual component level? Will you be legging into the spread? Will it be sent as a complex order?

- What is the maximum allowed loss?

- Is the expected return within the underwriting parameters?

- What is the target profit for this trade?

- What is the size for this trade?

- Does it conform to the position sizing parameters?

- At what point would the trade require adjustment (if any)?

- Do you know the possible adjustments to make to the trade (if needed)?

During the trade:

- Has the trade hit an adjustment point?

- Has the trade hit the profit/loss target?

After the trade:

- Did you log the trade in the trading diary?

- Did you follow the trading plan?

- If you did not follow the trading plan, why not?

5

The Trading Plan

"Failing to plan is planning to fail."

—Alan Lakein

Not every business has a business plan, but every successful trader has a trading plan. To make money consistently, you need a plan giving yourself a framework, defining the parameters, and keeping your focus.

Having a plan is not a prerequisite to starting a business. However, having a plan is usually a precursor to creating a *successful* business. Many people can start a business. The number of startups per year is large; but, in the end, only the ones with a plan that can be implemented well will survive and flourish. In the business of trading, successful traders have a trading plan that they follow. The reason for creating a trading plan is to guard against the emotional swings that you go through when trading. The trading plan establishes a framework. It gives you as a TOMIC trader a process to follow. The trading plan describes what to do in each scenario. It is like a flight plan and an emergency plan in one.

The trading plan contains guidelines for trading. It defines how you plan to play the game. In trading you make your own rules, but the key is to be consistent. If your rules do not work, get new ones, create a new plan. However, the only way you will know whether they work is by sticking to the plan and evaluating your performance continuously.

When a casino sets up a blackjack table, it gives its dealers specific parameters to follow when dealing cards to its clients. For example, the dealer must stay on 17 and must hit (take a card) on less than 17. This is a specific rule that the casino imposes on the dealer to have consistency across the casino, and it is done so that the casino has an edge. A trading plan works the same way; it gives the trader a framework to generate a consistent outcome. The trading plan gives you a chance to win by following a process providing measurable outcomes that can be improved continuously.

The Mind-Set

The mind-set of a successful manager of TOMIC or of any business is very important. When a U.S. Marine goes into the battlefield, he knows that he is fighting for his country and that no matter what, he won't be left behind. Marines can go into any scenario confident that their fellow marines are watching out for them.

The feeling of confidence in a trading plan is what you need to manage the TOMIC portfolio. The belief in the trading plan keeps you out of trouble and leads to profits consistently. However, confidence or belief in the plan is not enough. Following the plan will get difficult at times. That is why, as the successful manager of TOMIC, you have to be dedicated, disciplined, bold, flexible, and humble.

TOMIC is a business, and it will take a lot of dedication and commitment to follow the trading plan to make profits. There will be a lot of ups and downs that will impact your management psyche. It is not an easy business. The market will constantly challenge you. However, the commitment to the business will overcome the emotional swings.

You will need to be extremely disciplined in order to follow the trading plan, making sure that the entries and exits are followed, and that the underwriting is done correctly. The discipline helps you overcome the emotions of trading. One of the biggest reasons that traders blow up their portfolios is not taking losses early enough. This is because the emotion of losing is so great that taking a loss is undesirable. Even though the plan will say to take the loss early to avoid a larger one later, the undisciplined trader will freeze. You have to be prepared for this so that when the time comes to take the loss, you actually take it and follow the trading plan.

As the manager of TOMIC, you also need to be bold and decisive. There will be times when opportunities abound and you must decide whether to take them. Then there will be times when you will need to not trade, when opportunities are scarce. Also, being bold allows you to make critical decisions at the appropriate time.

Flexibility is one of the most underrated characteristics of a good TOMIC manager, but one of the most important. Being flexible together with boldness allows you to change course when things are not going your way. Let's say that you have a portfolio leaning net long and the market has reversed and gone from a bull to a bear market. You need to make the decision to change the portfolio from leaning long to leaning short. This is not easy to do if you are not flexible and decisive.

One more important characteristic of the successful TOMIC manager is humility. The market will send many curveballs. It is very unlikely that you will have 100% successful trades every year. Remember, even Warren Buffett has had his share of bad investments; for example, Salomon Brothers, US Airways, silver (way before silver took off in 2010–11). However, think of bad trades as learning opportunities. Bad trades provide feedback that teaches you how to do better next time. Being humble is the key to not taking losses personally. Losses are part of the business. If there were no losses, no one would need to insure and then TOMIC would be out of business.

In conclusion, your mind-set as the manager and trader is the key. You need to be dedicated, disciplined, bold, flexible, and humble in order to be successful at TOMIC. If you have a strong mind-set, you will succeed.

When a trade goes against you, be prepared but do not panic. Fortunes are made and lost in times of great uncertainty. Mental toughness is required in this business. It is like the great champions in sports, Michael Jordan and Tiger Woods. They have the mental toughness to be disciplined and come through at the end. It's the same in trading: You must have the worst-case scenarios planned out so that when something happens you don't freeze and you know what to do. Just like a commercial airline pilot, in case of emergency you calmly go through your checklist. An example of having a plan was that of Captain Chesley B. Sullenberger, who had to ditch a US Airways jet in the Hudson River in Manhattan on January 15, 2009, when the plane was hit by a flock of Canadian geese. Fortunately, Captain Sullenberger had trained for emergency situations, and he had a plan he was able to execute perfectly. In so doing, he saved the lives of all his passengers. Having a trading plan will help you have the scenarios mapped out and will give you that guide of what to do in an emergency.

The Importance of Sticking to the Process

When you're running a business, what do you think is better: sticking to a process or going with your gut? Being lucky or being good? The saying goes, "It is better to be lucky than to be good." However, you can't be lucky all the time. So, where does that leave you?

Assuming that you know how to play blackjack, take a look at the following scenario. You are dealt a 10 and an 8, making your count 18. The dealer is showing a 6. Potentially, the dealer could have a 16, in which case he would have to draw a card and probably bust. You hit (ask for a card) and fortunately get a 3, making your hand 21, a winner. There are high-fives all around the table and you think you are a great gambler. If you had been your TOMIC manager, would you have been happy with what you did? Hitting on an 18 with the dealer showing a 6...was that a good move? Even though you won, did the outcome justify the risk you took?

In reality, being lucky works great, if you are lucky all the time. However, the move you made at the blackjack table was a lousy move. The odds of your busting (losing) were very high if you drew a card, while the odds of the dealer having a 16 and having to draw were very high also. The dealer had a good chance of busting. So you should have stayed and let the dealer draw instead. You had a much better chance of winning if you had stayed with 18. Taking the hit was a bad (one could say stupid) decision. Hey, you won. But we absolutely would not hire you to manage our money. You won because you were lucky. But do you think that over the long run you would continue winning by making those kinds of decisions?

Here at TOMIC, it is extremely important to stick to your investing process. When you see good trades that give you a winning edge, you do them. It does not mean you will win every time, but over the long run you will win more times than you lose. You will not make trades where you perceive no advantage. You will not be the blackjack player hitting on an 18 because you feel lucky. Sometimes it may appear that others are winning and you are not in the game. Sometimes you will be playing when nobody else is playing. But, over the long run, you expect to win more than you lose.

So do you measure the outcomes or the process? To be successful consistently, you need to follow the process. However, you know that outcomes are important, too. Over the short term, process takes precedence over outcomes, but in the long term the outcomes take precedence over the process. If you stick to your investment process, even though on the short term the outcomes may show losses, over the long term the outcomes should show wins. Otherwise, if you don't win over the long run, the process will have to be changed. Going back to the blackjack example, you will not hit on 18 when the dealer shows a 6. You might lose sometimes, when the dealer actually has a 6 and a 5 to make 11 and hits it with a 10. But over the long run, staying on 18 will win more times than lose.

Process matters. Use a checklist, a list of things you have to check before you do something or in order to do it well. Did you know that before an airplane takes off, the pilot goes through a preflight checklist? They ask things like, is there enough fuel to get to where we are going? A very critical question, don't you think? A checklist is a process. This is what the trading plan gives you, a process.

Did you know that a checklist (having a process) saves lives?

Dr. Peter Pronovost, a physician-researcher at Johns Hopkins, developed a simple five-item checklist that saves lives.

In the article "Infection Rates Drop as Michigan Hospitals Turn to Checklists" that appeared in *American Medical News* on March 8, 2010, we can see the benefits of using a checklist by a group of Michigan hospitals. The article says that catheter-related infections have been a commonplace complication in the sickest patients in intensive care units and were responsible for around 17,000 deaths annually. According to the article, the cost for caring for an infected patient is $45,000.

The Michigan hospitals implemented a simple five-step checklist and were able to reduce their catheter-related infection rate by 66% after one year. They reduced their central-line infection rate to zero per 1,000 catheter days versus the national average of 5.2 infections per 1,000 catheter days. Their checklist contained five items: washing their hands, using-full barrier precautions when inserting the catheter, cleaning the skin with chlorhexidine, avoiding certain areas for insertion, and removing unnecessary catheters.[1]

The following is an excerpt from the article "A Basic Hospital To-Do List Saves Lives" that appeared in the *New York Times* on January 22, 2008:

> Using the checklist, in 18 months the average I.C.U. at these diverse hospitals reduced its catheter-related infection rate to zero, from 4 percent. All told, the checklist saved more than 1,500 lives and nearly $200 million. The program itself cost only $500,000.[2]

A simple five-item checklist that helped medical practitioners in an intensive care unit to follow a process saves lives. Amazing. Do you think a checklist for your investment decisions will save and make you money? It sure will.

At TOMIC you follow a process; that is why you have a trading plan. You have a checklist for the different functions at TOMIC. In underwriting you have a process for trade selection and risk management. Also, for executing a trade you have a process. Each step has a checklist to help you avoid making mistakes. You will not hit on an 18 when the dealer is showing a 6. You are disciplined and you take your job seriously. You are the casino, not the gambler. When you trade, odds are in your favor. You have winning and losing trades, but your process helps you to stay disciplined in order to make sure you win more than you lose.

Questions Your Trading Plan Should Answer

Every TOMIC manager has a trading style, just as every car driver has a different type of car (SUV, sedan, sports car, minivan, and so on). Each driver has a cruising speed they are comfortable with and a route for getting from point A to point B. However, every driver is governed by a set of traffic rules in order to avoid accidents. For example, there are different speed limits for highways and for school zones.

A TOMIC manager sets his own rules, his own "speed limits" that he self-regulates using a trading plan. The objective of a trading plan is to provide specific parameters to assist you when you are trading. Like the speed limit for the driver, the trading plan should give the TOMIC manager a set of guidelines and boundaries for his trading.

Every trading plan will have different parameters that are important to the trader and should answer some common questions. The following is a list of questions that you should answer in your trading plan:

- What is the goal of your TOMIC?

- What markets are you going to trade?

- Which strategies are you going to use?

- What are the conditions needed to put on a trade?

- What are the conditions that will make you close a trade?

- What are your risk management parameters?

- How are you going to execute the trades?

Try to answer the questions with as much detail as you can. Be specific. Ask yourself more questions, and answer them. Here are some more questions that come to mind:

- **Goals:** What is the goal of your TOMIC? Is your TOMIC designed to replace your current income? Is it your goal to make consistently 20% annual return on your capital? Is TOMIC a tool for learning to trade options? Is TOMIC supposed to always produce positive returns no matter what the market does?

- **Strategies:** What strategies will you be using in your TOMIC? Will you be using only theta positive trades? Or will you do both theta positive and theta negative trades? Will you be primarily trading iron condors, butterflies, calendars, and so on? What are the three strategies you are most comfortable trading and under what conditions? Which strategies should you avoid and under what conditions?

- **Entry parameters:** For each strategy you have decided to trade, what are the conditions you need for you to enter the trade?

- **Exit parameters:** What are the conditions, winning or losing, that would make you exit a trade?

- **Risk management:** What are the conditions for making an adjustment? Do you have safety limits set? What are your risk thresholds? What do you do if a position loses more than 2% of your portfolio's equity? What do you do if your portfolio loses more than 6% in a month?

- **Trading journal:** What information will you be keeping in your trading journal? Is the information that has been recorded enough to provide insights into the trading decisions when doing an after action review? Will you be using any special software to keep your trading journal?

Answering these questions will help you construct your trading plan. Create your plan, use it, and revise it as you grow. No trading plan is set in stone, but it is the first "stone" that you will need to build a successful TOMIC. In Chapter 10, "Operating the Business: Putting Together TOMIC 1.0 from A to Z," we walk you through a sample trading plan.

Endnotes

1. Kevin B. O'Reilly, March 8, 2010, "Infection Rates Drop as Michigan Hospitals Turn to Checklists," *American Medical News,* www.ama-assn.org/amednews/2010/03/01/prsa0301.htm, retrieved October 2, 2010.

2. Jane E. Brody, January 22, 2008, "A Basic Hospital To-Do List Saves Lives," *New York Times,* www.nytimes.com/2008/01/22/health/22brod.html?pagewanted=print, retrieved October 2, 2010.

6

Trading Infrastructure

The trading infrastructure consists of the back office elements needed to implement TOMIC. This includes but is not limited to risk capital, the broker, trading platform, analytical software, portfolio margin, information sources, dedicated space, and backup plans.

Risk Capital

TOMIC's trading infrastructure begins by defining how much money you will need to start the business. TOMIC is a scalable business. It could start as a small operation and grow into a larger one without your having to change much. What really changes are the skills of the operator.

Every business starts off with some capital, whether it is a lemonade stand, which has to have some capital to buy the lemons, sugar, and ice, or The One Man Insurance Company, which needs capital to cover its margin requirements. The margin requirements are the equivalent of the reserves of an insurance company. For an insurance company to be allowed to write insurance, it has to have reserves so it is able to cover any claims against the insurance it writes.

What is the right amount of risk capital to start with?

Depending on your plan, you could start TOMIC with as little as $5,000. If you are just starting out, plan for a small account, and add to it as you gain experience and consistent profits.

Depending on you as the operator of TOMIC, the levels of risk capital which you could start out in TOMIC are these:

Level 0—Beginner	$5,000 to $10,000
Level 1—Intermediate	$10,000 to $100,000
Level 2—Semiprofessional	$100,000 to $500,000
Level 3—Professional	$500,000+

Level 0—Beginner: A beginner is an operator just starting the journey into trading options. You are learning the basics on trading options, sending orders to the broker, and you know enough to place and take off a trade. Beginners should start with a small account allowing them to trade small lots and gain experience. Some brokers offer "paper accounts" that allow you to paper trade, meaning you can simulate your traders with fake (paper) money. The CBOE also has such a virtual site. The paper accounts are helpful for learning how to use the trading platform. However, they are not helpful for learning how to operate TOMIC. The stress from decisions made with real money is very different from the stress you get with paper money. As a beginner, you should start with a real money account.

Level 1—Intermediate: The intermediate operator is one who has a good understanding of options basics and knows the anatomy of the different trade strategies (butterflies, condors, calendars, and diagonals, for example). You understand the uses of the strategies and have some idea of trade selection and how to apply trades in different environments. You know enough to get in trouble, and enough to get out of trouble most of the time.

Level 2—Semiprofessional: Semiprofessional operators have more experience under their belt. You have good mastery of option strategies and know when to apply each. You know what trades give the best risk/reward ratio. You know how to trade and make adjustments. You are at a point where you know how to make money. You manage TOMIC on a part-time basis and have another job or are retired. A good portion of your income is derived from operating TOMIC. You are a master at managing trades.

Level 3—Professional: The professional operator operates TOMIC for a living. All or most of your income is derived from operating TOMIC. You might have TOMIC funded personally or might be managing other people's money in TOMIC. You manage the entire portfolio. That means that in addition to managing the individual trades, you manage the risk of the entire portfolio. You manage the Greeks not only of individual positions, but of the entire portfolio. You know how a trade impacts the Greeks. You are like a general in a battle; you manage the entire battlefield. Usually, your portfolios are larger and they have more trades on than the Level 0 to Level 2. One more thing: Your returns are not necessarily higher than those of the semipro traders, but they are more consistent. You know how to operate TOMIC to a level that delivers consistent returns. By managing the portfolio, you can smooth out the peaks and valleys, allowing for more consistent returns.

The Trading Platform (Broker)

A good trading platform is essential, especially when you are trading options. The One Man Insurance Company depends a lot on the trading platform. The ease of entering and executing an order is of paramount importance given that there is only one person at the helm. The One Man Insurance Company does not have a trading desk staffed with traders who take your orders and make sure they get done. You are the trader at the trading desk. You are also the underwriter, the chief executive, and the janitor of the entire company. Having a good trading platform will save you time and prevent costly trading errors.

Before we review the platform, a word about brokers. Here are some of the characteristics you should look for in an options broker:

1. *Option specialist:* A lot of brokers allow you to trade options; however, you should look for a broker specializing in options. This is important because it impacts the tools that they offer and the margins they provide.

2. *Understanding of complex order margin:* If brokers specialize in options, they offer better margin terms. For example, some brokers require margin for both sides (vertical credit spreads) of an iron condor. Good brokers will require margin for only one of the vertical spreads of the iron condor. If they know about options, they know that in an iron condor you can lose on only one side. Therefore, they need the margin equivalent for only one side of the iron condor.

3. *Customer service:* This is something we all want, expect, and deserve.

4. *Reputation:* Use a broker who gives you confidence that the firm is not going to go out of business. Make sure brokers are members of FINRA and SIPC.

5. *Trading platform:* The broker should have a good online trading platform that allows you to trade options easily.

6. *Trading desk:* In addition to the trading platform software, the broker should have a trading desk. This is for the times when the platform is down, or the Internet is down, or you need to call a real person for help.

After you have selected a set of brokers, you'll need to see which platform works best for you. The platform influences the broker you choose, unless you have a larger account and can afford to have a third-party platform to interface with your broker.

What is important to have in a trading platform? There are subjective elements like "ease of use" that are left to your discretion. Here is the checklist of what a good platform should have:

1. *Trade analysis tools:* This consists of graphic capabilities to plot risk graphs to analyze an option trade.

2. *Charts:* The platform should have some basic charting capabilities that will allow you to analyze the underlying market.

3. *Easy to use:* The platform needs to have an easy-to-use interface. Most brokers have a paper trading platform that you can try out before signing up.

4. *Customizable layouts:* Everyone is different and sees things differently. You should be able to customize the layouts of the information, which helps you speed up your data gathering and decision making.

5. *External links to Excel:* This is not a "must have" feature, but it is very useful. You can program spreadsheets in Excel and get real-time data from the platform. This gives you the flexibility of running calculations in Excel and is useful when you're looking for trades and monitoring your positions in real time.

In most cases the platform is broker-related. However, if you start managing a significant amount of money, say over $1 million, then third-party trading platforms that are broker agnostic may be preferable. Examples of third-party platforms are Obsidian, Derivix, Microhedge, and Real Tick.

Portfolio Margin

Almost all option brokerage accounts offer Reg-T margin. Therefore, if you have an account that allows options trading, you should be familiar with Reg-T margin. Reg-T was the only choice available to retail customers up until 2007. After 2007, some brokers began offering portfolio margin (PM) to retail customers. Each broker has his or her own account minimum requirements for portfolio margin accounts.

Portfolio margin is another way to calculate the margin requirement. Instead of calculating the margin on each individual position like Reg-T and then adding up the numbers, portfolio margin calculates the margin requirements over the entire portfolio. To calculate portfolio margin, the broker stress-tests the portfolio and calculates the margin required based on the outcome of the stress test.

What does having portfolio margin mean for TOMIC? It means that it has access to much more leverage. Here's an example of Reg-T versus PM on a married put:

Sample Position:

Long 100 Shares AAPL @ $330

Long 1 Put AAPL OCT 320 @ $18

Reg-T requirement:

50% of Equity Purchase Cost ($33,000) = $16,500

+

100% of Put Premium = $1,800

Total Reg-T Margin = $17,300

PM Requirement:

Maximum loss down 15% in stock = $4,950

–

Equity loss offset by theoretical gain in put options of $3,950

Net loss = $1,000

Total PM = $1,000

The difference between having PM and having Reg-T was $16,300. This $16,300 is capital liberated if your TOMIC had PM with no change whatsoever in the risk profile of the account. Not every position experiences such dramatic savings in margin. However, this example shows the significant difference you could have with PM versus Reg-T margin.

If your broker is more conservative, that will add additional "haircuts" to the standard portfolio margin requirement. For example, a broker could increase the requirement if the portfolio is too concentrated in one industry sector. So, when looking for a broker who offers PM, make sure you understand the broker's PM requirements.

One cautionary note: Just because you have PM does not mean that you have to use it to the maximum. Having PM gives you more flexibility, however. When managing TOMIC, you should always be aware of how much exposure you have and actively manage your risk. If you are a beginner, use the more conservative Reg-T standards until you are more adept at managing risk for your entire portfolio.

Information Resources and Other Analytical Tools

In this Internet age, it is easy to get overloaded with information. There are many hundreds of Web sites that help you gain perspective about what is going on in the world as you trade and manage TOMIC. Here is a list of sites that have been useful to us:

> **www.bloomberg.com**
>
> **finance.yahoo.com**
>
> **www.seekingalpha.com**
>
> **www.stocktwits.com**
>
> **www.thestreet.com**
>
> **www.theflyonthewall.com**
>
> **www.tradethenews.com**
>
> **www.livevol.com**
>
> **www.cboe.com**
>
> **www.ivolatility.com**

Some sites are free, some charge. Explore and find the ones most useful to you. This decision depends on the kind of trader you are and the products and markets you trade.

In addition to general market information and the tools provided by the broker, you can opt to use third-party providers for data and other analytical tools to help you improve your trade selection and risk management.

In some cases analytical data provided by your broker might not be as good or reliable as you want. For example, the Greeks provided are based on the model defined by the broker. Some brokers simplify (or become lazy) and don't include all the variables to calculate the Greeks. They might not use dividends in their calculation of the Greeks. This might not seem to be a big deal, but for some professionals it is. Hence, you may opt to buy data from a provider who does calculate the Greeks using models with which you are more comfortable.

Other useful tools are programs to view and analyze volatility skews and term structures. Tools similar to livevolpro.com or ivolatility.com are useful for selecting trades.

Another useful tool is a simulator, or back trader. This tool tries out new strategies and simulates the behavior and risk management adjustment to be used in your trades. This is good for traders trying to create systems; they are less useful for discretionary traders. Brokers like Thinkor-Swim have backtrading tools integrated in their trading platform. Also, you may purchase software packages like Optionvue, which has been a popular option backtrading tool.

Dedicated Space

Nowadays, you probably do not think that having a dedicated space for trading is important. Some people claim that they can trade from anywhere in the world given a notebook computer and an Internet connection. That might be true, but it does not work that well if you are trading for a living. It is helpful to have a dedicated work space where you can run your option trading business. It could be an office outside of your home, or a home office, or even a desk in your basement. It should be set where you can concentrate and focus without distractions.

Your trading space should be a place that

- Is quiet and allows you to concentrate
- Is free of interruptions, such as screaming children or vacuum cleaner noises
- Has high-speed Internet
- Is comfortable
- Provides a calm and serene environment

Backup Plans

When trading for a living, make sure that you have backup plans. You need redundant systems built into your infrastructure. Here is a list of things to consider in your backup plan:

- Have redundant Internet connections, from your cable provider, cellphone provider, or phone provider.

- Have a battery backup for your computer.

- Use at least two brokers.

- Use at least two computers, a primary desktop and a backup notebook.

- Have your broker's trade desk programmed on your speed dial or cellphone in case your trading platform fails.

- Have a futures account to be able to buy or short S&P 500 futures. Know how many S&P 500 deltas you own in the portfolio so you can go flat by selling or buying these futures.

- Have a backup location to go in case your office becomes unavailable (due to burst pipes, gas leaks, power outages, or air conditioning failures, for example). It could be a Starbucks, Barnes & Noble, a library, a hotel, an airport lounge, or any place with Internet connectivity.

Having a backup plan is important even though you probably won't need to use it, but occasionally you will be glad you have one.

7

Learning Processes

"It is not the strongest of the species that survives, nor the most intelligent that survives. It is the one that is the most adaptable to change."

—Charles Darwin

A s a successful TOMIC manager, you have to be able to learn and adapt as the business environment changes. Every successful business receives feedback. The feedback is from customers, employees, competitors, and suppliers. The truly successful businesses use this feedback to continuously improve. To create continuous improvement in your business, you need to embed a learning process into your business DNA. There are several elements you can use to instill a learning process. As TOMIC's manager, you need a trading journal, a sounding board, and a continuing education plan.

The Trading Journal

Every successful business has good records. Every good trader also has good records. This is a prerequisite to operating TOMIC successfully. Why are good records important? Because they provide feedback; they help your business keep score.

You have heard comments like, "A trading journal? Seriously, isn't that a waste of time?" A trading journal is a good use of time. In American football do the teams keep score? Do their coaches tape the games to analyze what the team does well and does wrong? How do the Dallas Cowboys prepare for a game if they don't know what they can improve from the prior game?

Anybody can trade for a short time. But not anyone can trade over a long period and be consistently profitable without feedback. Why do most good companies keep going and going and going? Why have good companies like Coca-Cola, GE, and Apple survived and flourished over the long haul? It is because they adapt to their marketplace; they change their strategies and adapt. Do you remember when Coca-Cola launched New Coke? It was a disaster; they changed the formula and got rid of the original. Their sales plummeted, and their competitors gained market share. What happened? They had to bring back Coke Classic. They were able to do this because they listened to feedback. The consumer of the original Coke did not like New Coke and stopped buying it. Coke noticed the drop in sales and quickly figured out that they had a problem.

Why do airplanes have "black boxes?" To record events leading to a crash so that they can be reported on CNN? No, it is for feedback. The only way the airplane manufacturers and airline companies can correct a problem on future airplanes is by knowing what happened in a crash.

Hence, coming back to The One Man Insurance Company (TOMIC), the trading diary is your black box recorder. It is designed to give you feedback and to improve your business. All the best traders, whether in stocks, options, or futures, keep a trading diary. A good example of keeping a trading journal is given by Dr. Alexander Elder in his book *Come into My Trading Room: A Complete Guide to Trading.*

What information is captured in the trading diary? Table 7.1 shows the data we suggest you should capture for each trade. You may add to this list any data that may be useful for you to measure your effectiveness as a manager of TOMIC.

Table 7.1   Data to Capture in Your Trading Log

Data	E.g.
Entry Date	11/21/2011
Exit Date	12/21/2011
Underlying Symbol	AAPL
Underlying Price at Entry	$372.00
Underlying Price at Exit	$390.00
Strategy	Short Vertical Spread
Price on Entry	$1.00
Price on Exit	$0.20
Margin Required for the Trade (Reg-T)	$9,000
Profit (loss) on the Trade	$800
Return on Margin (% over margin)	8.88%
Days in Trade	30
Volatility of the Underlying on Entry	30%
Volatility of the Options on Entry	28%

These are variables that you need to monitor constantly. It is useful to set up an Excel spreadsheet to monitor the positions you have in TOMIC. The Excel spreadsheet should include a real-time data link so you can monitor your positions.

Once the trades are closed, keep the information in your trading journal. Analyze your cumulative results monthly, quarterly, and annually. This gives you a sense of how you are doing. Also, pick a benchmark index to compare yourself against so you can tell whether you are doing well relative to the environment you are working in.

For example, answer the following questions:

1. How many trades did you enter this month, quarter, and year?
2. How many trades were profitable?
3. How many were losing trades?
4. What was your win rate?
5. What were your average days in the trade?
6. How much was your average win?
7. How much was your average loss?

8. How much did you win or lose on average per trade?

9. What is your average yield (realized profit/margin used) per trade?

Table 7.2 is an example of a summary table with the analysis of the monthly trades done at TOMIC. The table shows the relevant data for tracking the performance of the TOMIC manager. The first row shows the number of losses, nine, the total value of the losses, $(15,445), and the average size of a loss, $(1,716). The second row shows the information for the wins, and the third row shows information for the total transactions. The win ratio (percentage of winning trades) is 94%, and the total capital risked was $1,833,878. The average days in trade (DIT) was 26, and the average yield was 3.6%, which results from dividing $66,417 / $1,833,878. If you annualize the yield, you get a 63.8% return.[1]

Table 7.2   Example of the Monthly Trade Analysis at TOMIC

Total	Averages	Total	Description
$(15,445.25)	$(1,716.14)	9	Losses
$81,862.45	$535.05	153	Wins
$66,417.20	$409.98	162	Total Transactions
		94%	Win Ratio
$1,833,878.21			Total Capital Risked
		26	Average Days in Trade (DIT)
		3.6%	Average Yield
		63.8%	Annualized Yield
Results 2/1/12 to 2/29/12			

Keeping track of your performance every month, quarter, and year will help you know if you are doing well or if you need to make adjustments to your trading. For example, let's say that your win rate fell to 90%—would you think you have a problem? Maybe, maybe not. If you check your average loss and you see it is $(500) and your average win is $500, you could say that you are actually better. Because even though your win rate has fallen from 94% to 90%, your $loss/$win ratio has also fallen from 3.2 to 1.0, and your actual expected payout increased from $0.75 to $0.80. Compare Tables 7.3 and 7.4.

Table 7.3   Win Ratio 94% and $loss/$win Ratio 3.2

	Average	Probability	Expected Payout
Loss	$(3.20)	6%	$(0.19)
Win	$1.00	94%	$0.94
		Total Expected Payout	$0.75

Table 7.4   Win Ratio 90% and $loss/$win Ratio 1.0

	Average	Probability	Expected Payout
Loss	$(1.00)	10%	$(0.10)
Win	$1.00	90%	$0.90
		Total Expected Payout	$0.80

The trading journal allows you to check your performance against the targets you defined in your trading plan. In this example, Table 7.2, the goal of TOMIC was to earn between 2% and 4% per month. Hence, assuming that most of the capital was invested, knowing that TOMIC earned 3.6% this month lets you know that you are hitting your goals. This feedback is important to you as the manager of TOMIC because you gain confidence and know that you are making good decisions. However, if you had not been hitting your goals, the feedback would have alerted you to make corrections to you trading.

Sounding Board

Trading is a lonely profession. It is important that you, as the manager of TOMIC, be grounded in reality. One of the key success factors of TOMIC is the underwriting skills of you as manager. To improve your underwriting skills, meaning trade selection, you have to be open to feedback. A way to obtain feedback on your trades is to have other people help. Having a set of people who understand what TOMIC is doing and who can give feedback and advice is useful and advances your skills greatly. There are several choices for how you can set up a feedback system. The two easiest ways are (1) joining a trading group and (2) hiring a trading coach.

Joining a Trading Group

Some people claim that they belong to the CNBC trading group. That is totally wrong; watching TV talking heads is not being part of a trading group.

Being a member of a trading group gives you a sounding board for trying out new ideas. The group also helps with accountability. Even though you are ultimately held responsible for all of your trades, the group helps remind you of your trading plan and keeps you on the reservation. Find a group with trading styles and background similar to yours.

Some questions you should ask yourself when choosing a trading group include the following:

- What are the goals of the trading group?
- How will the interactions be? In person, online, by phone? Will you be using a chat room online (for example, Skype, AIM, Google Talk, and so on)?
- How often will you be meeting?
- How many members?
- What are the experience levels of the members?
- If everyone is a novice, will it be a case of the blind leading the blind?
- If there are different experience levels in the group, will the more experienced members be willing to share with the less experienced?
- What do you bring to the group?
- Does the group keep a meeting log? If they do, review it to see what they have been working on.
- Do you pool resources?
- Does the group have a coach?

Hiring a Trading Coach

A trading coach is someone you hire to listen to your trading strategies. The coach helps hold you accountable and helps you constantly improve on your trades. The coach is someone who is more experienced and has a wealth of knowledge and experience to share with you.

Some questions you should ask when hiring a trading coach include the following:

- What can I learn from this coach?

- Can the coach provide references? Talk to the people that have used his or her coaching services.

- How available is the coach? How easy is it to contact the coach if you get in trouble?

- How much time will you be interacting with the coach per week?

- What is the communication medium that you will be using? Nowadays, using an online meeting service like Webex or Gotomeeting is common.

- Does your coach know enough to challenge you? Will he constantly challenge you to improve?

- Is your coach an individual or part of a larger coaching organization?

- Does the coach have "student" trading groups that you could participate in?

- Does the coach still actively trade real money? How is his performance?

- How good are his/her communication skills?

Continuing Education

No matter what profession you are in, there is always something you can learn to improve your business. All highly skilled professionals— medical doctors, dentists, lawyers, computer engineers—have to keep up with their fields. They do so by attending seminars, going to classes, and pursuing continuing education.

As the manager of TOMIC, you too should follow a continuing education plan to stay at the cutting edge of options trading. Continuing your education and improving your skill sets are necessary to survive in the options trading profession. You should always be learning new things in order to be prepared for any event. It is like a karate practitioner who knows how to block and punch really well. He could probably defend himself with just blocking and punching; however, learning how to kick helps him have alternatives to cause damage to an opponent. The same principle applies to the manager of TOMIC. You should be skilled and fluent in all the different option strategies. You should know how to read the environment to use the best available strategy for the market conditions. You should always be learning.

Your education plan should include reading books, attending seminars, taking special classes, or joining coaching services like OptionPit.com. See Appendix A, "Recommended Reading," for a list of recommended books to continue your education. Also, you may find information on OptionPit.com services in Appendix C, "OptionPit.com."

Endnote

1. To annualize the yield, most people make the mistake of dividing the yield by the number of days and then multiplying by 365. This is not correct. To annualize the yield correctly, use the following Excel formula: $(1+\text{yield})\wedge(365.25/\text{number of days})-1$.

8

Understanding Volatility

Y ou are probably aware of how the pricing model works. To fully understand how to trade options, potential hedge fund traders need a strong understanding of how options function.

All option pricing models are very different. The older ones like Black-Scholes and the Whaley model are somewhat antiquated, but much like automobiles or houses, even the most advanced models rely on a certain amount of fundamental information. All models need five factors: underlying price, strike price, time to expiration, cost of carry, and forward volatility. Four of the five are pretty simple...and then there is volatility. To a hedge fund trader (and all traders, for that matter), volatility is by far the number one determinant of success. Forward volatility is the only factor that traders do not know.

Any educator, coach, book, software, or service that ignores volatility, or does not emphasize volatility as the primary and fundamental key to success, is likely not worth much. If you are unfamiliar with the concept of volatility, stop reading this book and grab a book on our suggested reading list. Even with a fundamental knowledge of what volatility represents, its practical application in and of itself is not an easy subject. This chapter explains the factors of volatility and what causes volatility to occur.

What Causes Volatility?

The model has to use forward volatility, but a majority of traders do not know what forward volatility is going to be. If you did know what forward volatility was going to be, there would be little reason to trade.

In fact, the uncertainty of volatility is your best friend. Traders who have a mastery of the subject will find that the road to success in an option hedge fund will be smoother. Mastering volatility does not mean that you need a sixth sense of some sort, but rather an understanding of how high or low implied volatility is moving.

Implied volatility is the measure of volatility that most retail and institutional traders track, but it is almost universally misunderstood. For starters, most traders do not understand what drives implied volatility. Commonly, the retail public thinks there is some sort of boiler room of market makers in which the trading price of the option is determined. The general assumption is that market makers set the option price and thus volatility. This could not be further from the truth.

Market makers may determine the market, and thus implied volatility, at any given moment in the markets they post. However, they do not, in the long run, determine the price of options. That is set through price discovery. If market makers place a bid too high for an option, the market will begin to sell these unmercifully to market makers. Traders have choices: eat a lot of options or lower the bid price. Once market makers have taken on a certain amount of risk at a given volatility level, they drop the bid price and lower their offer. This is done as a way to manage inventory, and volatility falls as a side effect.

If market makers overcompensate for a deluge of sales in an attempt to manage inventory, it will not be long before they start to see bids for those options. Pretty soon, market makers will be forced to raise the offer price in an effort to not sell too many options at too cheap a price relative to where they just purchased. Traders raise their offers and implied volatility increases along with it.

Table 8.1 shows an example of how this happens in a streamed market.

Table 8.1   Sample of How a Market Maker Might Move Markets as Customer Paper Flows

Trade	Bid	IV	Offer	Trade
100 at 1.10	1.1	30	1.2	
100 at 1.05	1.05	29	1.15	
100 at 1.00	1	28	1.1	
	0.9	26	1	100 for 1.00
No trade	0.95	27	1.05	No trade

Notice that market makers move their bid lower and lower. Then once the price of the offer drops to 1.00, traders find bids on the other side of their trade. This is the market makers' sign that the bid/offer has dropped too much by moving to 26% implied volatility. Realizing that the market is telling them that volatility is oversold, market makers quickly raise the bid price.

The determinant of implied volatility is not market makers, but supply and demand for options. Market makers take the other side of public orders, and those orders determine the market. The smart hedge fund manager can take advantage of market makers much the way the buyer did in the previous example, or better yet, take advantage of volatility the way the seller did in the example, in which the best trade across the board was the first sale of 100 at 1.10. Since TOMIC has the ability to initiate, it should look for opportunities to sell the overvalued contract.

Implied volatility is determined by the market, not the market makers. Selling when others are buying and buying when others are selling is the key to success. Smart hedge funds take the risk away from those who are panicking, or those who are overly complacent.

Three-Dimensional

Volatility might seem simple, but it is not, because "vol" is not a one-dimensional concept. It is actually three-dimensional. Traders using volatility to determine price have to look at all facets of options: the ATM options price in the near term, volatility skew, and term structure.

ATM Options

The most active options traded at any given time are almost universally front month ATM options. Trading in these options determines the overall structure of volatility in a product. Think of ATM options as sails powering a boat. While other parts of the boat affect speed, the effect of wind on the sail means more, not to mention the size of the sail and its angle against the wind. Movements in ATM options affect the price of OTM puts, OTM calls, and the entire term structure.

If front month ATM option IV is dropping, so will months further out. On the flip side, if IV is rallying, so will all other parts of the product's structure. Front month does not have the most "vega." However, front month options are far more sensitive to changes in implied volatility. The TOMIC manager will find that this sensitivity is why front month options are the number one determinant in the success of a trade, even if you don't hold ATM options. Because it has what is sometimes called "vomma"—the greatest sensitivity to changes in implied volatility—you will find that watching ATM front month options will indicate how IV on any option will move.

Skew

Skew, sometimes called "kurtosis," represents how different options' volatilities relate to each other in any given contract. There are several types of skew; however, within equity and equity index options, options usually have an "investment skew," where OTM puts have a higher implied volatility than ATM options, and OTM calls have a lower implied volatility than ATM options. Although there are occurrences in which this is not the case, most notably in deal stocks, FDA announcement stocks, and VIX options, equity options have an investment skew.

The main reason for this skew is found in the drivers in the equity marketplace: natural longs. What do most 401(k)'s invest in? Mutual funds are for the most part long stocks. What do most people have in their personal accounts? Most individuals hold long stock. In fact, if you want to get short in a personal account, there are all kinds of extra forms, questionnaires, and margin requirements you have to meet. The entire structure of the market is set up to make it easier to buy stock, and harder to short stock.

So what does this have to do with options? There are two main ways the general public hedges long stock positions:

1. They buy puts.

2. They sell calls.

If a large portion of the market has the same trade, and everyone is trying to buy puts and sell calls, it causes a demand shift. Puts will get bid up and calls will get depressed. This phenomenon has to be priced in somehow, and it shows up in volume. So the main reason for skew is actions by the general public.

Using Skew

Like ATM options, order flow determines how skew moves up and down. If there are too many traders buying or selling relatively low-priced OTM puts or low-priced OTM calls, IV can go "out of whack." This allows traders to set up trades that are statistically favorable. An overly flat skew may be the biggest determinant of success of a butter-fly. It also will typically lead to more successful back spreads and front spread trades. On a more basic trade you may only want to sell OTM put or call spreads.

By buying an oversold option or selling an overbought option in a "credit spread," you will be able to squeeze up to an extra .02 to .10 in and out of the spread. If you can save .10 on every 10 trades, you would save 100 in every trade. That more than pays for the typical commission cost, and in an active account an extra 100 per trade quickly adds up. Doing the math, a fund trading 500 contracts per month saves up to $5,000.

The relationship of skew is a complex one, and has a major effect on your success; you need to monitor skew. On a strike-by-strike, trade-by-trade basis, you should examine the curve before trading. Find the mispriced option if there is one.

For index traders, the solution is more complex. You need to do two things: On a global scale pick a few OTM puts and OTM calls using either percentage OTM or, better yet, delta, and monitor how these options are related to each other. For instance, if a 10 delta put trades 30% and the ATM option trades 20%, the 10 delta put trades at 150% of

ATM. As the 10 delta IV put moves up and down, you will be able to see how the relationship of the two also moves. Combined with monitoring ATM IV, you should have a good grip on how the curve appears.

For those trading index credit spreads, monitor the relationship of the entire curve. You will be able to squeeze a few pennies out of every trade. Although this is impossible to do by looking at a trading platform, programs that map the curve pay for themselves and are worth the investment.

Units

You need to be aware of the way OTM options price in terms of volatility. At a certain point an option stops behaving with volatility and begins to trade for a "price." In other words, an option that costs .10 on the SPX does not have volatility; it has a lottery ticket price. Although the chance of .05 to .10 options becoming worth anything is slight, the risk of these options cannot be overstressed. A .10 option that moves to 15.00 returns 1,500%, and there is no way to price that degree of movement in an option. Option pricing models were not designed to price the "human risk." We call "human risk" the concept that traders are not willing to sell extremely cheap options naked because of the risk of catastrophic loss. Although the first and second standard deviations are fairly priced, once a stock or an index moves past a two standard deviation, which is more than the pricing model predicts, options will move to that fourth or fifth standard deviation. Therefore,

1. Never short options worth .10 or less.

2. If you are short an option worth less than .10, it is probably worth buying to close even if there is a commission for that closing purchase.

3. A hedge fund that sells premium should always be net long these "units."

By following these three rules, you avoid a total catastrophic loss and may find yourself sitting on a surprise profit in the event of a major upward or downward move. An investment in 5% to 10% of the fund in option insurance will in the long run pay out.

Term Structure

Much like skew and ATM options, various contract months will see different amounts of paper. The further you go from the near term, the less liquid contract months become. Thus, a big order can move one month substantially relative to another month. Although overall volatility is important to the success of a calendar spread, you will find that by monitoring the relationship of different expiries, you open up an opportunity.

If a contract month sees an inordinate amount of paper flow, you should be able to take advantage of the movement in the relationships. If the near term is underpriced, it will make sense to buy near term and sell long-term options against it. The retail public should avoid this trade, but be aware that when this condition occurs, a long calendar is a losing proposition. When the near term is overpriced, it makes sense to sell the near term and buy the back months against it.

Front month options have much more sensitivity to IV changes than back months. The best opportunities to trade calendar spreads are when the front month becomes overpriced or underpriced in a quick move. Some traders make a living by simply trading "vomma" action of front month options against long-term options.

The price action in front months can also be used in a more general sense. If you would like to simply sell iron condors, butterflies, and strangles, monitor volatility relationships against each other. When the IV of one month becomes overbought, it makes sense to move a condor or strangle trade into that overbought contract month. It can also be a hint that you can avoid buying or selling a different contract month.

There are a few pitfalls you need to be aware of when "volatility swapping" or moving contract months, especially in individual equities. Be on the lookout for the following:

- Earnings
- FDA announcements
- Corporate actions
- Dividends

Everyone likes selling expensive and buying cheap, but a spread caused by any of the preceding actions can be a good reason to leave that contract month alone. In addition, if a spread is exorbitantly wide, even if the TOMIC manager thinks there is no reason for the spread, there probably is a reason. Do additional research, make phone calls, and dig into the message boards. If a swap seems too good to be true, it probably is.

Don't be afraid to trade swaps and different contract months against each other. The months are correlated but not tied. If you take advantage of these movements between months, you will see that there are higher odds of success than the pricing model predicts.

Volatility and the Model

IV is an *output* of the model, not an input. The Greeks are an output of the model and so is IV; so traders sitting in front of a screen have little power to control the risk outputs. If you are not managing your own volatilities, you cannot see your risk parameters. To properly manage risk, one should model how the Greeks and profit and loss will move across a wide variety of situations. You should also know what the IVs are of every contract you own. By knowing this, you can circumvent many of the pitfalls of retail trading platforms.

To monitor volatility, keep track of the following in every stock traded:

> ATM IV
>
> Skew
>
> Three-month term structure

For positions held, keep track of the following:

> The IV of every contract held
>
> The Greeks of the entire positions
>
> Expected Greeks
>
> Profit and loss based on a decline or increase in IV of 5%, 10%, and 25%.

9

Most Used Strategies

In this chapter you'll find the five most used strategies for TOMIC. This gives you an overview and an example of each strategy.

How should you set up each of the major short premium spreads? What is the exact criterion for evaluating a decent sale of insurance? Clearly, not all sales are equal and the key to any kind of success is to sell insurance premium when it is at a "good price." In this section you'll find five of the major spreads, from construction to management to exit. Although every trader has a different approach to trading, you have spent time studying each spread, trying to find what you believe is the best approach to trading them. The issue is that every trader has different risk tolerances and trading goals, so you need to think of the following as guidelines, not rules. As you build your insurance business, plan on tweaking and adjusting these guidelines. You are constantly attempting to improve and tweak your approach. As conditions change, parts of your overall strategy will have to be adjusted.

The Vertical Spread

Vertical spread is the general term for a bull call spread, bull put spread, bear call spread, or a bear put spread. The name *vertical spread* really derives from traders looking at an option montage and seeing that the spread is made up of the different strikes that are laid out vertically.

The vertical spread is one of the building blocks of other more complex spreads like the iron condor and the butterfly. If you were to get stranded on a desert island and could trade only one strategy, the vertical spread would probably be your choice. It is a spread that many beginners use because it is familiar to them. Many beginners start out with the covered call or naked puts. The vertical spread might consist of a short put combined with insurance or a short call combined with insurance. Most traders use it for directional plays, either bullish or bearish.

By definition, a vertical spread is composed of a long and a short option at different strikes in the same expiration.

Vertical spreads can be bullish or bearish and can be bought for a debit or sold for a credit:

	Bullish	Bearish
Debit	(1) Vertical call spread	(2) Vertical put spread
Credit	(3) Vertical put spread	(4) Vertical call spread

(1) Vertical call debit spread = long call strike < short call strike

(2) Vertical put debit spread = long put strike > short put strike

(3) Vertical put credit spread = long put strike < short put strike

(4) Vertical call credit spread = long call strike > short call strike

Here are the situations in which to use the different vertical spreads:

Bullish

(1) Vertical call debit spread: Use when partially bullish and don't mind theta decay.

(3) Vertical put credit spread: Use when partially bullish and want positive theta.

Bearish

(2) Vertical put debit spread: Use when partially bearish and don't mind theta decay.

(4) Vertical call credit spread: Use when partially bearish and want positive theta.

Focus on the credit spreads: the vertical put credit spread (bullish) and the vertical call credit spread (bearish). These spreads are theta positive. Assuming that there is no movement in the underlying, the trade earns money as time goes on.

Conditions

The vertical spread is best when you have an opinion on the direction of the market.

Volatility rule: Use vertical credit spreads in times of stable or declining market volatility. The width of the spread depends on the steepness of the skew. In steep curves, narrower spreads are recommended so the long option volatility has less of a gap with respect to the volatility of the short option. If the skew is less steep, you may use wider spreads to save on commissions.

Time: Usually place vertical spread trades with 30 to 60 days to expiration. This depends on how far out-of-the-money the spread is placed. On far OTM spreads the theta decay is more linear, so when you're doing longer trades, as in an iron condor, starting a trade 30 to 60 days from expiration is optimal.

Vertical Spread Example

Here is a vertical put credit spread on AAPL (Apple). On October 13, 2011, 30-day implied volatility and 10-day historical volatility were 38 and 37. IV was greater than HV, which is within normal parameters for this trade. Next, check IV, which was trending down from 51 on October 4, 2011. A falling IV is a good environment for this vertical spread.

You placed the vertical spread on October 13, 2011, at 10 a.m., when AAPL was trading at $405, shorted 10 AAPL NOV 360, and bought the 10 AAPL NOV 350 for a credit of 1.55 per spread, net $1,550 for the trade. See Figure 9.2 for the details. The risk profile of the trade can be seen in Figure 9.1.

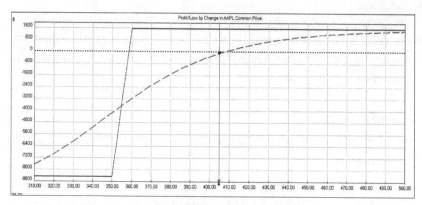

Figure 9.1 Risk profile of the 10 NOV 360/350 vertical put credit spread.
(Source: OptionVue6)

Options	NOV <37>					
405 calls>	MktPr	MIV	Trade	Ex.Pos	Vega	Delta
400 calls	22.45	38.9%			50.8	58.2
395 calls	25.35	39.3%			49.7	62.3
390 calls	28.45	39.9%			48.1	66.3
385 puts	11.45	39.6%			46.1	-29.9
380 puts	9.90	40.0%			43.8	-26.3
375 puts	8.50	40.5%			41.2	-23.0
370 puts	7.25	40.9%			38.4	-20.1
365 puts	6.15	41.3%			35.5	-17.5
360 puts	5.20	41.7%	-10		32.6	-15.1
355 puts	4.35	41.9%			29.6	-13.0
350 puts	3.65	42.5%	+10		26.7	-11.1
345 puts	3.05	43.0%			23.9	-9.41

Figure 9.2 Opening details of the 10 NOV 360/350 vertical put credit spread.
(Source: OptionVue6)

On November 4, AAPL was at $401 or below the price when you sold
the spread. However, IV was down. Implied volatility of the AAPL NOV
360 put was at 41.7% when you sold, and on November 4, 2011, the IV
of the AAPL NOV 360 put was at 34.1% (see Figure 9.3). The spread at
this point was worth $0.25. You had captured 83% of the credit received
so you closed the trade and booked the profit. You bought to close the
spread for $250. You sold the spread for $1,550 and bought it to close
for $250, resulting in a $1,300 profit for this trade.

Options	NOV <15>					
	MktPr	MIV	Trade	Ex.Pos	Vega	Delta
410 calls						
405 calls	6.60	25.0%			32.2	48.9
400 calls>	9.30	25.9%			32.3	59.0
395 calls	12.40	26.7%			30.8	68.3
380 puts	2.23	29.6%			21.5	-13.0
375 puts	1.57	30.3%			18.3	-9.75
370 puts	1.16	31.6%			15.3	-7.32
365 puts	0.85	32.7%			12.8	-5.50
360 puts	0.63	34.1%		-10	10.6	-4.15
355 puts	0.49	35.7%			8.74	-3.13
350 puts	0.38	37.4%		+10	7.20	-2.38

Figure 9.3 Closing details of the trade 10 NOV 360/350 vertical put credit spread. (Source: OptionVue6)

The Reg-T margin for this trade was $8,450 and the profit was $1,300. This gave you a return on margin of 15.4% in a span of 22 days.

The Iron Condor

The iron condor consists of two vertical spreads, both set up out-of-the-money: a short call spread set above the current price of the underlying and a short put spread set below the money. The goal of the iron condor is to set up the shorts at a distance the underlying is unlikely to get to over the life of the spread. For a primer on iron condors, you can refer to Jared Woodard's e-book *Iron Condor Spread Strategies*.

Conditions

Volatility: For an iron condor, implied volatility does not need to be high, but only higher than the average true range (ATR)[1] of the underlying. Thus, an iron condor can be traded in just about any type of volatility condition. It only matters that expectations of implied volatility are higher than ATR. Essentially, you think implied volatility is too high.

Iron condors are most effective in lower volatility. In higher volatility you are getting a higher premium or setting up the iron condor wider, but often ATR is high. The key to trading iron condors in high volatility is to try to sell when volatility is stable or falling, not when implied volatility is simply "high."

For example, on August 5, 2011, the CBOE volatility index was trading over 25%, historically elevated. However, that volatility was actually low relative to what the market was about to do. If you sold an iron condor in those conditions, you might have been considered selling "high vol" but you were not selling volatility that was too high. There is a major difference. In the case of August 2011, volatility was high, but it was on an uptrend, not a downtrend. An iron condor sold on August 5 would have had some major problems.

An iron condor sold only one month earlier would have been a different story. The VIX was not nearly as high as it reached on August 5, yet because volatility was declining, an iron condor would likely have been a quick exit for a trader who entered a spread.

Volatility rule: Stable or declining market volatility are key to a successful condor.

Skew: If you were simply selling strangles, the skew curve might be the most important part of the trade equation. Because you are selling an iron condor, thus selling a short and buying a long against it, skew seems to matter less. Still, it can help the trader recognize red flags.

In low volatility, typically, you would prefer a slightly steeper skew. Below ATM, an elevated skew will push the short slightly further away from ATM. Above ATM, the short call spread will receive slightly more credit. This is not of major significance, but it does matter.

An overly steep curve should be considered a major warning sign. When implied volatility has yet to rally, but the curve has caught a bid, this can be a sign of an impending volatility spike. Selling an iron condor into rising volatility is a recipe for disaster. Skew tends to be very steep in two instances: rising volatility and falling volatility. If IV is really low and skew is steep, either don't enter an iron condor or back up the truck on insurance.

Time: In Jim Bittman's book *Trading Options as a Professional* (a great primer for this book, by the way), one of the most compelling points in the whole book has to do with decay. There is a flawed belief that option time premium decays exponentially across all strikes in the final 30 days of an option's life. This is completely flawed; in the final 30 days, studies show, only ATM options decay exponentially. As price moves further away from at-the-money, options decay much more linearly. Jim points out that for an option 10% out-of-the-money, the option loses more value from day 60 to day 30 than it does day 30 to day 1.

Upon further study, options seem to have a "cone of feasibility" that relates to when and how they decay. As an option moves from being logically in-the-money to an option that cannot end up in-the-money, this is when options give up the bulk of their value.

Thus, when trading an iron condor, you should set up the trade when it will logically lose the bulk of its value. You will prefer to set up in the 10–15 delta range when creating your iron condor. Thus, under almost every circumstance, right around 60 days seems to be the optimal time to sell an iron condor.

Insuring: The greatest danger to an iron condor is not found when volatility is low. The greatest danger is not when volatility is high. It is during the transition from low to high when iron condors can completely destroy a TOMIC. The proper implementation of unit puts can save a portfolio.

The transition from low to high can ramp up the value of OTM puts. Thus, if volatility is in the lower 25% of its historical range, you should always spend a few dollars on insuring the value of the open iron condor. Although traders vary in how much they buy, no more than 10% of the credit received on a sale is necessary to ensure that the iron condor is properly insured.

On the other hand, when volatility is at its highest levels and declining, insuring may be unnecessary; it is likely that the trade was entered when you had a full view of the risk associated with the trade. It is also likely that any insurance bought would be ineffective, as the far OTM puts will already have a large portion of risk premium built into their price.

The setup: Once you have determined that volatility is "too high," you should look to sell a 10–11 delta call and buy the next call strike. However, this is not set in stone. A smart trader examines strikes around the 10–11 deltas to see whether there are any strikes that are mispriced. I have seen situations in which an SPX 1350–1360 call spread netted more than an SPX 1340–1350 call spread. This is generally due to a "public order" being in the "book." Then you should look to sell the 10–12 delta put against the call spread. You may cheat up a touch on the put side of the curve to increase credit and help flatten delta. Skew naturally causes the short put spread to be further away from the current trading price than the short call spread. Although stocks do "creep up and crash down," cheating puts in a strike or two does not make a profound difference in the outcome of the spread, especially if you insure the iron condor.

The return should be as such that you are getting good "odds" before ensuring. For instance, if you can get 2.00 on a 10-point spread, that equates to a risk/reward of 200 over 800, or 25% return on risk. If the trade has an 85% chance of success according to probabilities, you are in a very favorable position. If the trade has only a 70% chance of success, you are in a far less favorable trade. Although probabilities and payouts are only a function of volatility, it is important to be aware of these risk/reward comparisons. By looking for the best spots to buy and sell in an iron condor, you might be able to squeeze a few points of probability out of the trade. In trading, every .05 counts; an extra .05 in a spread might be enough to cover insuring the portfolio or pay for a commission.

Goals: A spread will almost never fully decay, and it almost never makes sense to allow a spread to fully decay. The goal should be to capture the premium sold as the trade left the "cone of feasibility." That amount is slightly over 50% of the value of the iron condor. Thus, you should try to collect about 55% of the value of the iron condor you sold. The intent is to be out of the condor by 30 days until expiration.

If the trade picks up 25% of the credit sold in under five trading days, you caught "edge" in the sale. You should exit the trade, stop, reevaluate current conditions, and then decide to enter a new trade if you are so inclined. Profit made quickly means there was edge in the trade, and edge should always be captured in a timely manner.

Risk: In managing risk, you need awareness of two types of losses: maximum loss and absolute maximum loss. Maximum loss is a number at which, once it's hit, you exit the trade. Set this number to equal your profit target, for example. In a given year you may expect to hit this maximum loss on one or two occasions. It is part of the business. However, if you manage the trade, the net of hitting several profit targets should result in a positive overall return.

In managing the trade a Third Third Third Rule is invoked: first adjustment at one-third of maximum loss, second adjustment at two-thirds of maximum loss, and exit upon hitting the final third of maximum loss. This is where absolute maximum loss is important. Absolute maximum loss is a number that you should never allow a trade to exceed. Set this number at the value of the credit received in the trade, for example. If at any point a 1.5 standard deviation move in one direction would put the trade beyond the absolute maximum loss, the trade should be adjusted or exited even if the trade is not yet at maximum loss.

In managing the risk, we are not fans of "rolling" out a trade. The kite spread, the ratio spread, the vertical spread, and the back ratio spread are much better adjustments. You will find examples of the kite spread adjustments in Appendix D, "Kite Spread." An iron condor is set with such a wide area that managing the underlying within that area is not that difficult. The idea of rolling out and increasing size can be costly, difficult, and risky. In more general terms the goal should be to get the most effective hedge and spend as little as possible. Like trades themselves, each adjustment is right for a specific circumstance. For quick reference here are a few guidelines for each adjustment:

Upside:

Kite spread: This is the primary adjustment for upside movement. This trade reduces gamma and costs typically very little. The one time this trade is not the optimal spread is when implied volatility is especially low. In just about every other circumstance this trade works.

Back ratio: This is the secondary adjustment on the upside. This trade also reduces gamma and costs very little. However, because of the structure of the trade, this should be used only in cases where the implied volatility is at very depressed levels.

Call spread: This is the trade of last resort when you need a lot of delta in a hurry. This makes sense only if you think the market is going to "roar" higher and implied volatility is extremely depressed. It is the quickest and easiest way to get a lot of delta. However, because of the cost, it should be avoided unless you are in a true pinch.

The margin trade: The time call spread is a great spread for those that have portfolio margin. It involves buying a front month call and selling a higher back month call against it. This is a great spread in many conditions and may become the preferred adjustment for TOMIC. However, because it is somewhat complex to trade, you should fully understand term structure before entering the trade.

The one-by-two call spread may also be a good trade, although typically it will create a debit on the upside. If traded properly, it can make money even if the market turns back.

Downside:

Ratio spread: When you expect volatility to rally as the market falls, the short 1 long 2 ratio spread can be a great way to manage this risk. It will not expand the trade out; however, it will quickly flatten the curve. This should be considered the primary adjustment for the downside if volatility is normal.

The put spread: Because of put skew, a put spread is a much cheaper option for an index trade than a call spread. This trade is a versatile, if still somewhat expensive, adjustment for the downside of the curve. This should be considered the secondary adjustment.

The margin trade: If you have margin, a one-by-two front spread makes a lot of sense. The trade is inexpensive, it sets a very wide tent, and unlike the other trades, when the market turns around, if entered properly, this trade adds to profit and loss.

Exit: When a goal is hit, good or bad, it is time to call the trade a day. It can be tempting to stay in a trade beyond your goal; however, discipline must trump "gut." We have seen more dollars lost on gut feeling than just about any other type of loss. When exiting, make sure to exit the entire trade including insurance. Those dollars and cents matter. If the long put purchased for protection is worth less than .10, keep it. The sale, after commission, is like a waste. We would also note that although adjusting may change margin, the trade's goals set from the original onset should not change. Adding or removing capital from the trade should have little to no effect on the net targets.

Iron Condor Example

On October 19, 2011, you evaluated the January contract month for a possible condor. You noticed that IV was trading at a premium to realized volatility, and you also noted that IV was trending lower. Skew was elevated but not off-the-charts high. You set the trade so that you were trading as much as you could along liquid strikes. You also received a favorable payout relative to the odds of success on the condor.

Collecting about 2.50, your goal was to make at least 1,250 and to be out of the trade by 30 days to expiration. See the iron condor details in Figure 9.4. The initial profit and loss risk graph of the iron condor trade is illustrated in Figure 9.5.

Options	DEC <58>					
1355 calls	MktPr	MIV	Trade	Ex.Pos	Vega	Delta
1350 calls	4.50	21.0%	+10		85.6	10.1
1345 calls	5.30	21.4%			92.2	11.2
1340 calls	6.10	21.8%	-10		98.8	12.2
1335 calls	6.80	21.8%			105	13.5
1330 calls	7.50	21.9%			112	14.8
1325 calls	8.60	22.3%			118	16.1
1320 calls	9.70	22.6%			125	17.4
1315 calls	10.80	22.8%			131	18.9
1000 puts	12.70	42.7%	-10		94.6	-11.7
995 puts	12.20	43.0%			92.3	-11.3
990 puts	11.80	43.5%	+10		90.1	-10.9

Figure 9.4 Opening details of the SPX 990/1000/1340/1350 iron condor. (Source: OptionVue6)

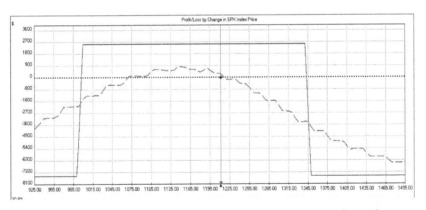

Figure 9.5 Risk Profile of the SPX 990/1000/1340/1350 iron condor at the start of the trade. (Source: OptionVue6)

Obviously, a slow grind down is the best scenario, but if IV came in and SPX rallied, you would have been pleased as well.

Over the next 30 days there were times when this trade got threatened. However, it never actually touched the Third Third Third Rule. After 30 days, your condor was up about 1,000 (see Figure 9.6). Not quite your goal. However, this was probably worth the exit considering the proximity to the top of the chart and your desire to be out of the trade by day 30.

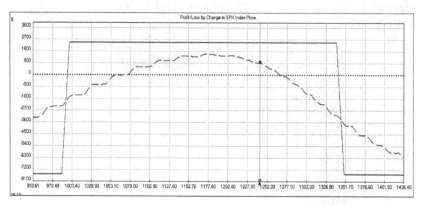

Figure 9.6 Risk profile and current P&L line (T-0) of the SPX 990/1000/ 1340/1350 iron condor at the close of the trade. (Source: OptionVue6)

Again, the setup made the trade. Adjusting can be tempting, but as with most trades, the key to risk management is trade entry.

The ATM Iron Butterfly

The iron butterfly consists of two vertical spreads, both at-the-money, a short call spread with the short ATM, and a short put spread set ATM. The goal of the iron butterfly is for the underlying not to move as the decay from the short ATM straddle outpaces the decay from the protective strangle set around the short straddle.

Conditions

Volatility: Much like an iron condor, for an iron butterfly implied volatility does not need to be high, but only higher than the average true range of the underlying. Thus, an iron butterfly can be traded in just about any type of volatility condition. It only matters that expectations are that implied volatility is higher than ATR. Essentially, for your iron butterfly you think implied volatility is too high. You will find that iron butterflies are much easier to manage in low-volatility environments than in high-volatility environments.

An iron condor is a play on how high implied volatility is relative to ATR, whereas an iron butterfly is a play on how high ATR is relative to how high ATR is going to be over the time period involved, along with high relative IV. This is because the iron butterfly is ATM and has a narrower wingspan. Even if ATR is low relative to IV, the fly can still lose if the underlying moves too far or if the underlying makes "gapping moves."

However, unlike with a condor, the final determinant of success for an iron butterfly is the overall relationship of the wings relative to the value of the straddle. More than any other factor, the final determinant of success for an iron butterfly is the skew.

Skew: An iron butterfly is basically a short straddle and a long strangle. The key to its success is going to be the price you pay for the strangle. This makes iron butterflies more successful in a low-volatility environment, as long as the relative relationship of the wings is inexpensive compared to the thorax or "meat" of the iron butterfly.

For equity flies the put often is either overpriced or underpriced. Your iron butterfly contains a "normal skew" and you need to know what that is. When the put trades over a 6% discount in IV terms, this is a favorable time to enter an iron butterfly. If it trades at a 10% discount to IV, this is an excellent time to enter the trade. When the put skew is flat, the trade will be a short and very likely profitable trade.

When the put is too low, if IV rises, the OTM put will skyrocket not only to a more normal skew but possibly even higher as the depressed put overreacts to market IV movement. This provides the trade additional padding on a spike. So losing trades will typically lose less. On the flip side, if IV does come in, the OTM put will probably not see its IV move as much in relative terms as the sinking ATM IV. When IV is falling, skew will rise, allowing the fly to outperform the pricing model's expectations in falling IV markets.

For example, in the SPX normally the 10 delta put trades at 140% premium to ATM IV. So if ATM IV is 20%, the 10 delta put will trade at about 28%. If that 10 delta put is trading at 26%, the skew of the put is too flat at 130% of ATM. One of three scenarios could occur:

1. If ATM increases to 22% and skew normalizes, the 10 delta put increases from 26% to about 30.8%, or almost 5%, as opposed to less than 3% it would normally increase. This should mute much of the IV spike from the ATMs.

2. If ATM IV declines to 18%, there is a good chance that the skew will normalize. This causes the put to drop from 26 to 25.2, almost nothing. You will be able to capture a larger portion of the IV move downward than the model predicts. This reduces the time you are in the market and lets you close out the spread on any downward IV move.

3. If ATM IV stays stable, there is a high chance that the put will increase in IV by 1% to 2% regardless. This places 1% to 2% of IV into your pocket. It will push you toward a profit target much more quickly.

The out-of-the-money call is typically less important than the put as it tends to move around less. The cheaper long call, the better, for the same reason. On top of this, when you purchase the call cheap enough, if the underlying rallies and IV comes in, you will find that the position acts the way you expected; this is a distinct advantage.

Skew rule: You want a *flat* put curve and a *steep* call curve, which is not as rare as you might expect.

Time: As the trade is placed ATM, it does make sense to put trades on inside of 30 days in an attempt to capture exponentially decaying insurance values. There is no "too close to expiration" rule, although the most experienced traders will not try to hold an iron butterfly into the final three or four days until expiration. Although the same IV and skew rules apply, the exploding gamma that comes with decaying insurance premiums can be a real challenge.

With the introduction of weekly options, there is considerable opportunity for you to smooth out returns by selling short-term iron butterflies in weekly issues.

Insuring: Typically an iron butterfly has a very tightly defined risk. Insurance should be a part of the overall portfolio. When IV is low, and especially if skew is flat, it pays off in the longer term to own one to two unit puts for every 10 iron butterflies sold.

The setup: Inside of 30 days, once you have found a product with stable or falling ATR, a stable or falling ATM IV, and a flat put curve and steep call curve, you probably have a good candidate. Setting up the iron butterfly is simple: Sell that ATM straddle. Buy the wings at a one standard deviation for the maximum number of days you want to be in the trade. For an iron butterfly with 30 days to expiration, this might be 15 to 20 days. Once the wings have been placed, you will be short delta; that delta should be flattened. Flattening the delta makes your trades volatility plays and not directional trades.

To flatten delta, buy a call or two *inside* the tent of the iron butterfly. Buying fewer calls closer to the money is a better way to flatten delta than buying many calls out-of-the-money, due to the predictability of returns for calls closer to the money. You might also flatten delta with stock or futures. Once the delta has been flattened, if you are going to buy a few units (which is advisable), this should be done now. The trade will end up flat delta, although the units bought might make the trade nominally short.

Goals: The goal of an iron butterfly is to get in and out as quickly as possible. A well-constructed iron butterfly makes 5% to 10% in only a few days if traded properly. Beyond 10% you are probably giving up your "edge" in the trade. Although it might be tempting to shoot for 15% to 20% return on an iron butterfly and hope that days pass with nothing going wrong, this approach is not a long-term way to make a profit. Thus, at 10% start locking in a profit. You can do this by employing a strangle-tightening technique.

Risk: Well-constructed iron butterflies are *very* easy to manage. Typically, if the trade gets outside of the tent, it should be about a wash. Exit the trade at that point. The key is to cut iron butterflies for a scratch when they break outside and keep winners profitable. Once an iron butterfly has reached the profit target again, take the trade off, or at least tighten up the strangle. Figure 9.7 shows an example of tightening the butterfly.

Once a trade is up 10%, typically the wings will have lost much of the long gamma they offer as protection; the current profit-and-loss curve will develop some shape and begin to look more like the iron butterfly at expiration. If you sell the far-out wings and buy wings inside, in effect buying an iron condor, you will find that you have completely flattened the profit and loss curve again. This is an excellent way to stay in the trade yet ensure that profits are locked. Once the strangle is tightened, if the day's profit-and-loss curve breaks the expiration tent, close up the trade and take the money out.

Original butterfly

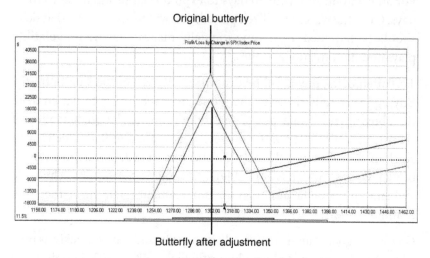

Butterfly after adjustment

Figure 9.7 **Risk profile comparing the original butterfly and the butterfly after the tightening adjustment. (Source: OptionVue6)**

Beyond tightening the strangle, there are not a lot of great available adjustments. However, a few are effective if you choose to actively manage risk aggressively.

Upside: One approach for nonmargin trading not involving buying or selling the underlying security is buying a call to clean up some of the deltas while at the same time tightening the spread on the downside of the iron butterfly. If the stock has rallied enough to threaten the top part of the iron butterfly, it makes a lot of sense to tighten up half of the strangle and buy a call. You might also use call spreads to achieve the same result.

For margined traders, much like with the condor, the call time spread and the one-by-two ratio spread work wonders in repairing an iron butterfly.

Under no circumstances should adding a butterfly be used as an adjustment unless you would execute that iron butterfly on its own. Although it will extend the trade, these iron butterflies are not add-on devices in the best of conditions and add a large amount of margin. Every major loss in iron butterfly trading that we have seen involved "tranching flies." In general we have found that throwing capital at a trade is not a long-term solution to making money in options.

Downside: A well-constructed iron butterfly will not lose if it breaks the tent to the downside. Your first choice should normally be to shut down the trade in those circumstances. In the event that you insist on staying in the trade, an iron butterfly will adjust very much like an iron condor.

Ratio spread: When you expect volatility to rally as the market falls, the short one-long, two-ratio spread is a great way to manage risk. It will not expand the trade out; however, it will quickly flatten the curve. This is the primary adjustment for the downside when volatility is normal.

Put spread: Because of put skew, a put spread is a much cheaper selection for an index trade than a call spread. This trade is a versatile, if somewhat expensive adjustment for the downside of the curve. This is a secondary adjustment.

The margin trade: If you have margin, a one-by-two front spread makes a lot of sense. The trade is inexpensive, it sets a very wide tent, and unlike the other trades, when the market turns around, if entered properly, this trade adds to profits.

Exit: Iron butterflies should make or lose 10% or less. If the trade "breaks out," it is probably a close. If the trade hits that 10%, the edge is gone and it's time to close or tighten.

ATM Butterfly Example

After Christmas, you notice that SPX skew is especially flat. This is not unusual during holiday weeks as few open positions equates to less insurance bought. This can flatten skew, especially when overall IV is average or high. You look up the deltas of the puts in Figure 9.8. Then you calculate the skew between the 10 delta puts and the ATM. Next, you refer to Figure 9.9 and look at the calls and notice the 25 delta call is also trading within range. You determine that now is the time to enter an iron butterfly. Notice the relationship of the 1270s and the 1170s.

1350 calls	MktPr	MIV	Trade	Ex.Pos	Vega	Delta
1270 puts>	25.20	18.5%			130	-50.6
1260 puts	21.00	18.9%			128	-44.1
1250 puts	17.70	19.8%			124	-38.1
1240 puts	15.20	20.8%			117	-32.7
1230 puts	12.70	21.5%			109	-27.9
1220 puts	10.70	22.2%			100	-23.7
1210 puts	9.00	23.0%			91.2	-20.0
1200 puts	7.40	23.6%			82.2	-16.9
1190 puts	6.30	24.5%			73.7	-14.3
1180 puts	5.30	25.2%			65.7	-12.1
1170 puts	4.20	25.5%			58.4	-10.2

Figure 9.8 Option montage with SPX put information. (Source: OptionVue6)

Calls are also in good shape. Notice the relationship between OTM calls and ATM options (see Figure 9.9).

Options	JAN <24>					
1320 calls	MktPr	MIV	Trade	Ex.Pos	Vega	Delta
1310 calls	6.40	16.1%			97.5	22.3
1300 calls	9.00	16.4%			111	28.7
1290 calls	12.70	16.9%			121	35.5
1280 calls	17.50	17.8%			127	42.4
1270 calls>	22.40	18.2%			130	49.3

Figure 9.9 Option montage with SPX call information. (Source: OptionVue6)

Next you calculate a 17-day standard deviation based on the 1270 strike (Figure 9.8 1270 puts) and an ATM IV of 18.5%:

$$0.185 * SQRT(17 / 365) * 1270 = 51$$

You round to 50, setting up the trade at 1220/1270/1270/1320 (see Figure 9.10 for details). With a delta of –28 you buy a call to flatten the delta. Then, like all smart traders, especially those trading flies in a flat skew environment, you buy a far-out-of-the-money unit put, as shown at the bottom of Figure 9.10. The trade risk graph is illustrated in Figure 9.11.

Options	JAN <24>					
	MktPr	MIV	Trade	Ex.Pos	Vega	Delta
1330 calls						
1320 calls	4.20	15.6%	+5		81.4	16.6
1310 calls	6.40	16.1%			97.4	22.3
1300 calls	9.00	16.4%	+1		111	28.7
1290 calls	12.70	17.0%			121	35.5
1280 calls	17.50	17.8%			127	42.4
1270 calls>	22.40	18.2%	-5		130	49.3
1260 calls	28.70	19.1%			128	55.8
1250 calls	35.10	19.7%			124	61.8
1240 calls	42.20	20.4%			117	67.2
1270 puts>	25.20	18.5%	-5		130	-50.6
1260 puts	21.00	19.0%			128	-44.1
1250 puts	17.70	19.8%			124	-38.1
1240 puts	15.20	20.9%			117	-32.7
1230 puts	12.70	21.5%			109	-27.8
1220 puts	10.70	22.2%	+5		100	-23.7
1210 puts	9.00	23.0%			91.2	-19.9
1120 puts	1.95	29.6%	+1		31.3	-4.52

Figure 9.10 1220/1270/1270/1320 SPX butterfly details. (Source: OptionVue6)

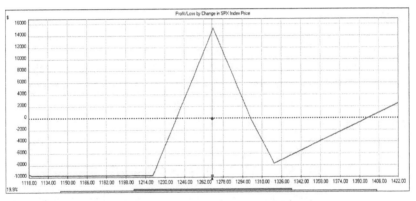

Figure 9.11 1220/1270/1270/1320 SPX butterfly risk profile at the start of the trade. (Source: OptionVue6)

Selling the iron butterfly at 41.35 (before adding in the wing and the unit), your goal is to return 5% to 10% in a few days. Recall that you margin off the fly, not the hedges. This should not be that difficult because the trade is at a favorable price.

While the stock does move up and down over the next few days, at no point is this well-constructed trade ever in any real trouble. On January 5 you are up almost 900, more than your 10% goal (see Figure 9.12).

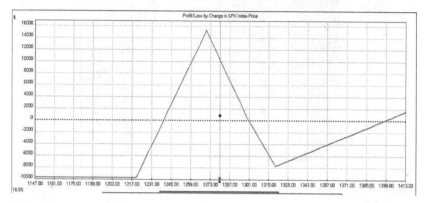

Figure 9.12 1220/1270/1270/1320 SPX butterfly risk profile at the close of the trade. (Source: OptionVue6)

If you had held one or two more days, you would have made a total killing with the trade, but you should never complain about taking a smart and disciplined profit. A smart setup with proper screening created an easy trade. You may have noticed a major pattern here. Well-constructed trades are easy to manage.

The Calendar Spread or Time Spread

The calendar spread, either short or long, can be the best trade a hedge fund can use. If you are saying, "I can't sell calendars!" remember how similar the S&P 500 futures options are to SPX options. They can offer an alternative when you want to sell time spreads. Unlike butterflies and condors, this spread relies on the relationship between options with different term dates traded off one another.

While a calendar spread can be an effective trade and is easy to explain, it is also the most sensitive to proper execution. Both long and short trades are excellent for any fund. To understand calendars, you need to understand the concept of weighted vega, the idea that the different months have different vegas but also have different sensitivities to changes in realized volatility. In a perfect world you would have a book of calendars, both long and short, with little to no positive or negative theta and with all the trades put on the perfect conditions. This would produce a portfolio of favorable trades in which the overall weighted vega was not overly high or low and protected your portfolio from huge swings.

Conditions

Volatility:

Long: For the long calendar spread, you usually prefer below-average implied volatility and very low realized volatility. In a perfect world you would see little to no movement but an increase in implied volatility at the same time. Although that might sound great, it *never* happens. In fact, if implied volatility is *too* low, the long calendar spread is likely to get beaten up on a pop in realized volatility. It doesn't matter what IV you buy; if the underlying market moves around, the calendar is going to lose. Therefore, you will find yourself in a much happier place if you buy normal volatility, not the bottom 15% of IV range.

Short: For the short calendar you will find there are two times when these work best: when IV is superdepressed, and when IV is very high. In both cases the breakout of the extremes makes the short calendar work so well. The key to the short calendar is to put it on when gamma is most effective. In the case of high IV, the combo of long gamma and IV coming in at the same time makes the short calendar a big winner coming off of high volatility. The long gamma in the trade offers you some protection against the market moving hard. On the low end, term structure comes into play on a calendar. Because front month options are so sensitive to change in realized IV, front month IV can move and the gamma can work without back month options moving. This is likely to happen when IV is extremely low.

Skew: Because both options are bought or sold, skew is not a major factor.

Term structure: A calendar spread, either short or long, is really a term swap in which you sell one month against another. Overall implied volatility, the spread between front month options and back month options, is going to be the number one determinant of success. The combination of the right IV and the right term structure makes trading both short and long calendars a layup.

Long calendar: The key to the long calendar is to sell the short at a higher level relative to the back month options. Take a look at an individual product monitor in which the IV relationship is between where front and back month options normally trade. Begin to sell the front month when it trades at a significant premium to the normal spread. A significant premium is at least 10% of front month IV (thus, if front month IV is 20, you want that front month trading at a 2% premium to the normal relationship). At the same time, make sure that IV is not out-of-control high. If it is high across the board, that can be a sign that there is an event coming. Another sign that there is something wrong is when the months are trading at too high a premium. Generally, if the front month is trading at a premium of more than 25% over the front month IV, look at why the relationship is out of whack (in fact, always be wary of a calendar if the months are out of whack). The key with a long calendar is to sell overbought volatility, not volatility that is high for a reason.

Short calendar: IV conditions that make a long calendar bad are the exact conditions that make a short calendar great. The contract month bought should trade at a 10% discount of normal ATM IV. Also be wary of an overly wide spread. The key with a short calendar is to buy oversold IV, not sell high IV.

Time: The rule applied to butterflies also applies to calendars: Trade them within 30 days of expiration. There are two exceptions. If IVs are out of whack, any contract month can be traded against another. So a contract with five months to expiration can swap against one with six, seven, or eight months, especially in ETFs or index funds. If one month is out of whack in the far-out months, it is likely caused by liquidity, not an event.

Trading a calendar in the final days of expiration is much more difficult to handle than a butterfly because of the way the gamma explodes against the back month options. Also, the IV relationships lose relevance in the last couple of days of trading. In the final few days of a contract's life, this has less to do with IV and more to do with absolute straddle price. Anything within one week to expiration is straddle price, not an IV trade.

The setup: For the long, sell an ATM call or put and buy an ATM in the next month out when the relationship is that 10% out of line. Once they are in line, unwind the trade. It is that simple. Pick the months and pick the strikes. Buy relative midrange IV and the trade is likely to succeed. Make sure IV has been stable. You do not want to try to catch a falling knife, but if IV is in the midrange and stable, that is a good long setup.

For the short, look for ultra-low overall IV or ultra-high IV and a spread in which the month bought is cheaper than the month sold. Once the spread moves into line again, close the trade. There are occasions when you can trade overall high IV and ignore the IV spread to some degree; however, this approach is for only the most experienced hedge fund trader.

Goals: The goal of the calendar spread is to make 5% to 10% in a few days. Going for any more implies you are closing your eyes and hoping that the underlying doesn't move, or that IV doesn't move against you. Hedge fund traders trade volatility, not theta decay of calendars. Get in, take the 5% to 10%, and get out. If the trade touches the breakeven at expiration, kill the trade. It is tempting to add to the trade, but you will likely be flat to slightly down. With a book of calendars, taking 10% and giving up less than 5% will lead to a profitable book of trades.

Risk: It almost never pays to add to a well-constructed calendar spread. Most big calendar spread losses are incurred when they are out of the tent and you add a bunch of time spreads to the trade. However, there are some chances to add to calendars or adjust, especially on the short calendar spread side.

If the long spread is still out of whack, you might add to the calendar as long as you flatten up the delta at the same time. To put an additional calendar spread on, conditions must be as good as or better than the original trade. If not, do not adjust using a calendar spread. In that case, you might buy an option to cut delta down, but make sure you buy the contract in the less expensive month.

On the short side of the trade, any move in the underlying should allow you to profit. However, as the underlying moves around, there is a chance that conditions will not change. If that is the case, you might have the chance to scalp long gamma. Consider using a "pay the decay" approach in scalping, but do this only in small incremental moves. If the market is moving less than a one-day standard deviation, once the underlying makes a run, unwind the trade; do not attempt to scalp gamma back and forth. Scalping gamma was created to defend against time decay, not as a way to actually make money. If the trade hits 10%, take the money and run.

Exit: Never lose more than 10% on the margin of the original calendar spread. Exit if that happens, and shoot for no more than 10% return on a calendar. If 5% happens in less than a day, consider it a gift and kill the trade.

Long Calendar Spread Example

Here is an example of a long calendar spread. On November 16, 2010, at 3 p.m., you noticed that the OEX December-January call spread provided a great setup for a calendar spread. Overall volatility was relatively low at around 19% (see Figure 9.13). At the same time, the December IV was, due to a minor market shock, increased in IV to the point that it traded at an IV premium to January.

Options	DEC <32>						JAN <67>					
535 calls	MktPr	MIV	Trade	Ex.Pos	Vega	Delta	MktPr	MIV	Trade	Ex.Pos	Vega	Delta
530 calls>	12.40	19.6%	-5		62.6	51.7	17.20	19.4%	+5		90.4	51.4

Figure 9.13 OEX Dec and Jan ATM implied volatility. (Source: OptionVue6)

You entered contracts selling December and buying January for 4.80. The ATM calendar had Greeks, as shown in Figure 9.14.

Delta	-1.67
Gamma	-1.84
Theta	30.63
Vega	139.0

Figure 9.14 ATM calendar Greeks. (Source: OptionVue6)

Your hope was that the spread would collapse and December would fall below January. Or that the spread would hold and January would creep slightly higher. The next day (Figure 9.15), your luck was even better. By 3 p.m., not only was December lower, but January was slightly higher.

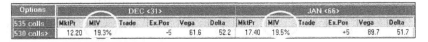

Options	DEC <31>						JAN <66>					
	MktPr	MIV	Trade	Ex.Pos	Vega	Delta	MktPr	MIV	Trade	Ex.Pos	Vega	Delta
535 calls												
530 calls>	12.20	19.3%		-5	61.6	52.2	17.40	19.5%		+5	89.7	51.7

Figure 9.15 Next day OEX Dec and Jan ATM IV. (Source: OptionVue6)

Overnight your trade made over 5%. This is exactly what you are looking for in a calendar spread. The point of the swap is not to hold for decay, it is to make money off mispriced volatility. The black dot in Figure 9.16 shows where your profit was as you unwound.

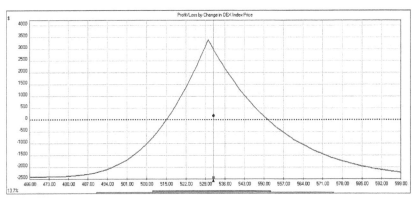

Figure 9.16 Profit and loss of the OEC calendar at closing date. (Source: OptionVue6)

Calendar spreads set up like this all the time. They might not always make 5% overnight, but if done consistently in the right conditions, over time, the banked edge will pay out.

Short Calendar Spread Example

When a long calendar spread looks bad, a short calendar spread can look great. On December 16, January options became greatly oversold relative to February options. At the same time, overall volatility was elevated. You entered a SPX Dec-Jan Short 1220 call spread taking a 1.6% volume credit and selling Feb at 24.4% IV. The net sale was 14.10 (see Figure 9.17).

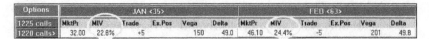

Options	JAN <35>						FEB <63>					
1225 calls	MktPr	MIV	Trade	Ex.Pos	Vega	Delta	MktPr	MIV	Trade	Ex.Pos	Vega	Delta
1220 calls>	32.00	22.8%	+5		150	49.0	46.10	24.4%	-5		201	49.8

Figure 9.17 SPX Dec-Jan Short 1220 call calendar at start of the trade. (Source: OptionVue6)

You were hoping for the front month to tighten up relative to the back month. For the relationship to hold steady, the underlying has to move and IVs have to hold, or some combination of these.

By December 20, the trade was a winner. While the front month did fall more, the underlying moved and the back month options sold off much harder than the January (see Figure 9.18).

Options	JAN <31>						FEB <59>					
1225 calls	MktPr	MIV	Trade	Ex.Pos	Vega	Delta	MktPr	MIV	Trade	Ex.Pos	Vega	Delta
1220 calls	42.90	22.7%		+5	139	60.8	56.30	23.8%		-5	195	57.7

Figure 9.18 SPX Dec-Jan Short 1220 call calendar at close of the trade. (Source: OptionVue6)

The trade can be bought to close for $13.40, a profit of about $0.80 in 4 days. You made more than 5% in just a matter of days (see Figure 9.19).

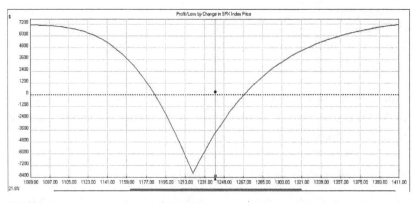

Figure 9.19 Profit and loss of the SPX short calendar spread at close. (Source: OptionVue6)

When you are patient, you do even better as the underlying keeps rallying. You could have made 20% on this calendar spread just by owning oversold options.

The Ratio Back and Front Spread

The ratio spread can be one of the best trades a hedge fund can apply. For those without portfolio margin, buying two and selling one is normally the only spread to use. If you have portfolio margin, look at buying one and selling two (often called a front spread).

The keys to the one by two, much like the butterfly, are skew and volatility. However, this spread adds a third component: direction. To succeed in trading ratio spreads, you need to be right on skew and volatility. For the spread to be wildly successful, you need to be right on direction as well, although you will find that this does not always have to be the case.

Conditions

Volatility: The ratio back spread is almost always a long vega spread at onset. The two long positions have a higher net vega weighted or unweighted than the one short, at least at onset. However, as time passes, that goes away if all other matters are equal. This is why when you're putting on a ratio back spread, the lower the implied volatility, the better. Never put on a ratio spread unless the IV is in the lower 40% of the current IV. Unless this trade is in a position where IV can go up, the trade is likely to not succeed without a big directional move.

Skew: Because you sell an ATM IV and buy two OTM puts or calls, the skew is going to matter. Based on the discussion in butterflies, the flatter the skew, the better. You hope to buy the curve at an extra cheap price. The cheaper the better, especially if IV is also low. You hope the general public recognizes that the OTM options are the cheapest and bids them up, even if IV doesn't also move. If IV goes up, the skew normalizes and the two OTM puts can do well. A pop in IV, skew, or both can get you out of a trade without the stock even moving. Add in being right directionally and you can make a killing on these spreads.

Be on top of IV and skew when trading ratios. Not taking this into account is throwing money down the drain on a ratio back spread. A steep skew and high volatility will cause these trades to lose even if you are right on direction.

Time: A ratio spread can be executed in any time frame. The key is to pick the right month, which has the lowest relative IV (at 60 days to expiration, compare the two-month option to the 60-day IV in the past). Adding in skew, this can make any month a winner. There are important issues to note: Trades executed close to expiration rely on the underlying moving, and trades executed further to expiration rely more on movements in volatility. If you make a directional bet and a ratio spread sets up nicely, use it. If you want to set up a ratio spread as a portfolio hedge or as a long IV play, use months with at least 60 days to expiration.

The setup: If the goal is to play volatility, the key is to get that same flat skew you wanted in a butterfly. You want the skew to trade 7% to 10% underpriced and IV to be in the lower 40 percentile of historical range. Sell one at- or near-the-money put or call, then buy two OTM calls or puts against, and the net premium paid for the two should be less than the value of the one sold. You want a credit or want at least zero cost. This way, if you are wrong on direction, you can still win from volatility. Do not go for a "big credit" but accept as little credit as possible. This will allow the two long positions to hang in for as long as possible.

Goals: When you're trading volatility, the goal is to get in, take the money, and get out. Ratio spreads are just like any volatility play. Your goal is about 10%, and you will never take more than 10%.

Risk: There are few adjustments that make sense for ratio spread. If the trade does not work out, close it. If conditions change for the better and the trade is losing, close the trade. If the trade is losing and conditions have made the trade potentially even better, add to it, assuming you have not overcommitted capital.

Exit: At 10% take the win or, at a minimum, lock it up. Never allow a trade to lose more than 10% of original margin. If the trade was added to, you might use that margin.

The one-by-two or one-long-two shorts: The one-by-two call spread is much like a calendar. The conditions that are awful for a back ratio are great for the one by two. One important difference: Make sure that the trade generates a credit. Unlike a ratio in which you want the trade to move in your direction, a one-by-two call spread is based on the underlying moving in the opposite direction. Once it moves away from the two shorts, the skew should flatten and IV should come in. At that point it is likely that the one by two sold at a credit can be bought to close for a credit as well. This is a sure sign that it is time to kill the one-by-two spread. As with any trade, you are not going for a home run, you are trying to make your 10%.

Ratio Spread Example

The ratio spread may be the easiest spread of all. On June 6, 2011, with the VIX near all-time lows, you determined that not only was IV low, but the skew was relatively flat with the 10 delta put trading at 135% of ATM. Realizing that skew is relative, you bought puts cheap. You were not sure the market was going to drop. Thus, you entered a ratio back spread selling the July ATM SPX 1280 puts and buying twice as many of the July 1230 puts (see Figure 9.20).

Options	JUL <39>					
1520 calls	MktPr	MIV	Trade	Ex.Pos	Vega	Delta
1290 puts>	30.60	16.2%			167	-52.6
1280 puts	26.20	16.7%	-5		167	-46.7
1270 puts	22.40	17.3%			163	-41.1
1260 puts	19.20	17.8%			157	-36.1
1250 puts	16.20	18.2%			149	-31.4
1240 puts	14.00	18.9%			140	-27.3
1230 puts	11.80	19.3%	+10		130	-23.7
1220 puts	10.10	20.0%			119	-20.4

Figure 9.20 July ATM SPX ratio back spread. (Source: OptionVue6)

The trade was long gamma, long vega, and slightly short delta. It also would not lose much if you were wrong and the SPX rallied (see Figure 9.21).

Delta	-2.77
Gamma	0.96
Theta	-145.1
Vega	461.5

Figure 9.21 July SPX ration back spread Greeks. (Source: OptionVue6)

The payout is shown in the graph in Figure 9.22. Your goal was for IV to rally and the underlying to fall at the same time. Because the curve was flat, your hope was that skew would also steepen, causing the 1290s to gain even more than the model predicted.

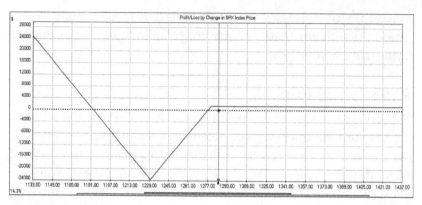

Figure 9.22 6/6 SPX ratio back spread profit and loss graph. (Source: OptionVue6)

On June 15, the trade started to make some decent money. The IV went up and SPX dropped as skew increased incrementally (see Figure 9.23).

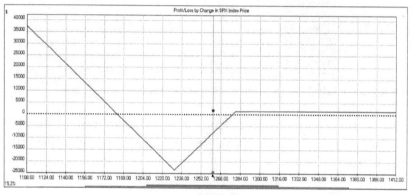

Figure 9.23 6/15 SPX ratio back spread profit and loss graph. (Source: OptionVue6)

You hit your goal, able to sell your spread at a decent credit (see Figure 9.24). You flip out of the position on June 16 up quite significantly. You didn't have any major problems because you set up your trade properly. Skew, time, and volume were all on your side.

Options	JUL <29>					
1300 calls	MktPr	MIV	Trade	Ex.Pos	Vega	Delta
1280 puts	38.80	19.8%		-5	137	-60.2
1270 puts	33.90	20.6%			141	-54.1
1260 puts>	29.70	21.4%			142	-48.2
1250 puts	26.00	22.1%			139	-42.6
1240 puts	22.80	23.0%			135	-37.5
1230 puts	20.00	23.8%		+10	129	-32.8

Figure 9.24 6/16 SPX ratio back spread exit the trade. (Source: OptionVue6)

The direction helped but was the least important part of the trade.

Endnote

1. Average true range (ATR): A measure of volatility introduced by Welles Wilder in his book *New Concepts in Technical Trading Systems.* ATR is a moving average of true ranges (generally 14 days of the true ranges). True range is the greatest of: 1) current high less current low, 2) absolute value of the most recent period's high less the previous close, 3) absolute value of the most recent period's low less the previous close.

10

Operating the Business: Putting Together TOMIC 1.0 from A to Z

I s there a secret sauce for making a successful option trading business? There is. One of the best books on learning to be a salesman is *You Can't Teach a Kid to Ride a Bike at a Seminar*, by David Sandler. As the title of his book conveys, you probably will not learn everything that you need if you don't trade. You will need to trade many times until you learn how to be consistent and make money.

In this chapter you'll find guidelines for operating TOMIC. To succeed at TOMIC, it takes commitment, dedication, and practice. So far, you have reviewed the ingredients. You have examined the most used trades: vertical spreads, calendar spreads, iron condors, butterflies, and ratio spreads. The question is how to mix all the ingredients to obtain a succulent meal. Review the recipe to be successful at TOMIC. Recall that the key success factors of an insurance company are these:

- Trade selection
- Risk management
- Trade execution

To do all three functions effectively, you also need to have your support structures in place:

- A trading plan
- Trading infrastructure
- A process for learning

In this chapter you will examine a sample portfolio for TOMIC 1.0. You will follow the decisions we take. There are many ways to cook a meal. Likewise, every portfolio is unique and every TOMIC is unique. There are many variables that depend on your comfort level and style of trading. The following is an example of TOMIC called TOMIC 1.0. As your skills progress, your portfolio evolves and becomes unique to your style of trading and comfort level.

Trading Plan

Every TOMIC begins with a trading plan. You should be able to answer these questions:

- What is the goal of TOMIC 1.0?

- Which markets am I going to trade?

- What are the strategies I will employ for each market?

- What are my risk management parameters?

- What is the best way to efficiently execute the trade?

Goals: TOMIC 1.0 is a portfolio used to learn and condition you as an option trader, into the framework of managing an option portfolio like an insurance company. The profitability goal is to not lose money over any 12-month period and to have an annual absolute return greater than 10%. The monthly goal is to make around 1% return on total capital.

Markets: You will follow a total of 10 markets, including indexes, ETFs, and equities. The markets you will follow are SPX, RUT, NDX, RTH, OIH, AAPL, CAT, EXC, MCD, and WMT.

Strategies: As you progress in proficiency as a manager of TOMIC, you will have more and more strategies in your arsenal. You will use different strategies for different market setups. However, for this example you will use just a handful of most used strategies. You will use the following strategies:

- Vertical spreads (credit and debit)

- Iron butterflies (and their variations, broken-wing butterflies)

- Iron condors (and their variations, unbalanced condors)

- Calendar spreads

- Ratio spreads

Table 10.1 shows the five strategies used in TOMIC 1.0 and the conditions in which to use them.

Table 10.1   Strategy Cheat Sheet

	Conditions	Volatility	Skew	Time	Goal
Vertical spread (credit)	Trader has directional opinion; IV is higher than HV	Stable or falling	NA	30 to 60 days	60% to 70% of the credit received
Iron condor	IV is higher than HV	Any IV level; falling	Somewhat steep	60 days	50% to 60% of the credit received
Iron butterfly	IV is higher than HV	Middle range; falling IV	Flat	10 to 30 days	Get out as quickly as possible with 5% to 10% gain
Long calendar	IV is low; good term structure	Relatively low; positive vol. structure	Not much impact	10 to 30 days	Get out as quickly as possible with 5% to 10% gain
Ratio spread	Trader has a directional opinion; IV is low	IV is low	Flat skew	30 to 60 days	5% to 10% unless trader catches a "runner"

Risk Management Parameters for TOMIC 1.0:

Maximum loss allowed per trade: 2%.

Maximum portfolio loss allowed per month: 6%.

Portfolio concentration limits: No more than 20% in any one industry sector.

Stay in cash if conditions are not favorable for any trade.

Trade duration: Less than 90 days.

Execution:

You will be using an online broker who specializes in options. The broker should have an easy to use interface for submitting complex trades (such as vertical spreads, condors, butterflies, or calendars). You won't require portfolio margin for TOMIC 1.0; a Reg-T margin account will suffice.

Setup:

- Start TOMIC 1.0 with $100,000.

- Keep a trading log in Excel.

- Use an Internet connection provided by your phone or cable operator and use the Internet connection from your cellphone as a backup.

- Use a laptop computer to trade, in case of a power failure.

- Program the broker's phone number into your cellphone with our account number in hand. If online access is down, you can call the broker by phone in an emergency.

Figure 10.1 shows an example of how your trading log looks for a vertical spread.

Trades	Adjust Date / Days in	Strike / Symbol	Units / Name	Open	Commissions / Graph / Alert	Debit/Credit	Mark / %Yield	Mkt. Value / Max Loss	Gain/Loss	Extrinsic / TTN	Delta	Theta	Vega	IV Start	IV Current	IV Change	Mark/Sale
	21	AAPL	APPLE INC COM			TTN	7.88%	$(1,485.00)	710.00	$ 693.00	0	0	0	39.94%	30.39%	-9.55%	
Vertical Credit Spread																	
AAPL 100 NOV 11 360 PUT	10/14/11	AAPL 111115P	-10	$3.080	2	$3,075.00	0.660	-$660.00	$2,410.00	0.66	$50.00	$110.00	$90.00	41.14%	34.31%	-6.83%	
AAPL 100 NOV 11 350 PUT	10/14/11	AAPL 111115P	10	$2.080	2	-$2,085.00	0.395	$395.00	-$1,695.00	0.40	-$30.00	-$60.00	$60.00	41.95%	37.37%	-4.58%	
		Net:		$1.000			0.265										
Insert Adjustments Below																	
AAPL 100 NOV 11 360 PUT	11/04/11	AAPL 111115P	10	$0.660	0	-$660.00	0.660	$660.00	$0.00	0.66	-$50.00	-$110.00	$90.00	41.14%	34.31%	-6.83%	
AAPL 100 NOV 11 350 PUT	11/04/11	AAPL 111115P	-10	$0.390	0	$390.00	0.395	-$395.00	-$5.00	0.40	$30.00	$80.00	-$60.00	41.95%	37.37%	-4.58%	1.01
Total				$0.00		$720.00		$0.00	$710.00		$0.00	$0.00	$0.00				

	Last	Change	%Change	Volatility % of 1SD	
Open Date					
Underlying Price at Open	$401.37	-$1.70	-0.42%	26.64%	30.39%
P.P. 85%					

Cash flow + 2 way comm.

T+ $1.00	T+ $7.00		Spread Vol	$10.00
			Cash Flow	$990.00
			Requirement	$9,010.00
			Current TN % of CF	70.00%
1 Std. Dev. 6.38%	$394.99-$407.75	$384.48-$418.26	Max Loss	$990.00
2 Std. Dev. 12.76%	$388.61-$414.13	$367.6-$435.14	150.00%	7.88%
3 Std. Dev. 19.15%	$382.22-$420.52	$350.71-$452.03	TTN -$1,485.00	$710.00
Closed 11/4/11				

Open Date 10/14 Strike $417.19

Set GTC for: 50.31
Set ML Alert for: $2.44
Set Adj. Alert for: 51.99

Figure 10.1 Example of an entry in the trade log of an AAPL vertical spread.

Executing the Trading Plan

You start out with $100,000, and monitor the markets you want to trade: SPX, RUT, NDX, RTH, OIH, AAPL, CAT, EXC, MCD, and WMT.

You know that you can risk up to 2% in each trade. This means that each trade should not risk more than $2,000 (2% of $100,000).

You will try to do at least three trades per month as long as market conditions permit.

Assume that conditions are right to do a vertical spread in AAPL. Let's walk thru the example in Figure 10.1. An AAPL vertical put spread consists in this example of ten points. The Reg-T margin is $9,010. Is this within the risk parameters of TOMIC 1.0? Yes. The $9,010 is the potential maximum loss the trade would have if no adjustments or actions were taken while in the trade. However, TOMIC 1.0 is an actively managed business, and part of risk management is adjustments you make during the trade. In this trade you place a "maximum loss" point at 150% of the credit received. In this example the credit received was $990 (including commissions), so your "maximum loss" is ($1,485). This means that if the trade got to the point of losing ($1,485), you would close and take the loss. This would represent 1.49% of the $100,000 fund, within your 2% risk per trade allowed.

Make sure that when you enter a trade conditions are right. Also make sure you know your exits. Know when to exit whether you are making money or losing money. Notice that in the AAPL example you had an exit of ($1,485) if you were losing money and an exit at $693 if you were making money. This trade was closed making $710 because you hit your target.

Have a mix of trades in the portfolio. Follow your markets every day and determine the best trades available given the conditions of each market. Have an opinion of the direction of the market. Follow the implied and historical volatilities of each market. This helps you determine the best trades available.

Keep track of the best available trades on a table. Table 10.2 shows an example.

Table 10.2   List of Best Available Trades

Best Available Trades Now: (Date)						
Market	Direction (Opinion)	Time Frame (of the Opinion)	IV	HV	Skew	Strategy Options
SPX	Up	30 days	20	25	Flat	Ratio spread, vertical spread
NDX	Up	30 days	35	32	Steep	Iron condor
RUT	Down	60 days	32	29	Steep	Vertical spread
RTH	Sideways	60 days	25	23	Flat	Iron butterfly
OIH	UP	60 days	22	25	Steep	Calendar, iron condor
AAPL	UP	30 days	42	35	Flat	Vertical spread
CAT	UP	30 days	25	23	Steep	Vertical spread
EXC	Down	30 days	21	20	Flat	Calendar, iron butterfly
MCD	Up	60 days	18	22	Flat	Vertical spread, short calendar
WMT	Sideways	60 days	15	16	Flat	Calendar

From your available trades, select the best to create a portfolio of trades. Try to create a balanced portfolio based on the overall market environment. Table 10.3 gives an example.

Table 10.3 TOMIC 1.0 Portfolio Example

TOMIC 1.0 Portfolio (Created from Selecting Best Trades Available)

Market	Trade	Debit / Credit	Margin Required	Max Loss	Profit Target	Time to Expiration	Prob. of Profit
SPX	Ratio spread	$ (443)	$24,558	$ (900)	$ 310	30 days	80%
NDX	Iron condor	$ (1,000)	$ 9,000	$ (1,500)	$ 700	60 days	80%
AAPL	Vertical spread	$ (800)	$ 9,200	$ (1,200)	$ 560	30 days	85%
EXC	Calendar spread	$ 11,000	$11,000	$ (1,320)	$1,100	30 days	45%
RTH	Iron butterfly	$ (3,400)	$ 8,600	$ (1,290)	$ 860	30 days	40%
	Total		62,358	(6,210)	3,530		
	Return on Margin			-10%	6%		
	Return on Assets Under Management			-6%	4%		

Notice that no trade had a "maximum loss" greater than $2,000 or 2% of the assets under management. If the portfolio lost more than 6% in the month, you should close all the trades in the portfolio and go flat. Then reassess your strategies and start fresh the following month. Your total target win for the portfolio was $3,530, which represents 4% return on AUM (assets under management), and your average of days to expiration was 36 if everything went to expiration. In reality, trades would be closed before expiration. In our experience this type of portfolio would have average days in trade between 25 and 30 days.

Once the portfolio is working and you hit exit targets on a trade, you should close the trade whether you are making money or losing money. When you hit your profit target, close the trade. It locks in profits and reduces your exposure.

Once you take off a trade, go back to the available trades list, and select the best available at that time and place it. Thus, you replace the trade you closed and keep TOMIC 1.0 making money. However, if the environment is hostile and there are no good trades available to place, do not place a trade. Wait until conditions are favorable before entering a replacement trade.

To become a proficient TOMIC manager, you must make trades. It is like being a heart surgeon: The more operations you perform, the better you become. Make sure to write your trading plan with as much detail as possible. Define your goals, risk parameters, strategies, and entry and exits parameters. Go ahead and execute the trading plan. Create a feedback loop. Keep a trading log with detailed notes to learn from each trade you make. At the end of each month, check your performance and see what you can improve on the following month. Repeat this cycle continuously, and you will become a better TOMIC manager.

11

Lessons from the Trading Floor on Volatility

Understanding Weighted Vegas in SPX Index Options

ark Sebastian wrote the following in his OptionPit.com blog on 12/06/2010:

> Some people call a calendar a good way to hedge the short vega from income spreads. This might be true in some cases but not in all cases. It is better to understand the movements of implied volatility across options. One should understand how volatility spikes affect volatility. The chart below is a graph of 30-day implied volatility (higher line) compared to 90-day implied volatility (lower line). What do you notice?

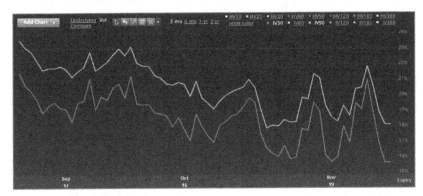

(Source: Livevol © www.livevol.com)

Notice how the 30-day is much more frenetic than the 90-day volatility. I call this the vega neutralizer. It is true that calendars are long, what we on the floor would call raw vega. However, traders need to remember that the movement in the front month can neutralize any movement in the back month options.

This extra movement in the front month is in many ways caused by the gamma of the spread. While the back month volatility is increasing, because of the long time to expiration, thus the price movements matter less. Meanwhile, in the front month, these crazy price movements can have a more permanent effect and can really move deltas of the spread around. This can make being short a lot of front month options a dangerous game. Traders need to compensate for this price movement.

On the floor the only way to do this was to jack up the front month implied volatility more than in the back month. Since back month options have more time to relax, we raised the vol, not wanting market to get too out of whack. But, if one remembers how much vega are in back month options, if things get really expensive, owning those suckers can be a very dangerous game. We were always afraid to own expensive back month premium because the IV coming in could be deadly, so we didn't raise the IV that quickly.

The same must happen on the way down; traders only have a limited time to get out of a losing volatility position, or a position where the underlying has stopped moving, especially when dealing with ATM options (we have all seen why; if not, see the following graph).

The action of the market halting causes the whole world (retail traders included) to sell premium pretty quickly. Traders on the floor who do not want to have to choke on premium kill the IV of the front month in order to avoid gaining too much inventory of long options. With more time for back month options to take advantage of another spike in market volatility, traders are not as quick to kill the back month options. We can clearly see this happening between the graphs below, which is the way the term structure looked on 11/30:

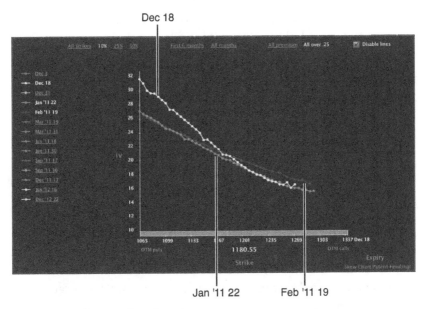

(Source: Livevol © www.livevol.com)

The following is today's closing vol. Notice how December and January implied volatility was sold off far harder than Feb:

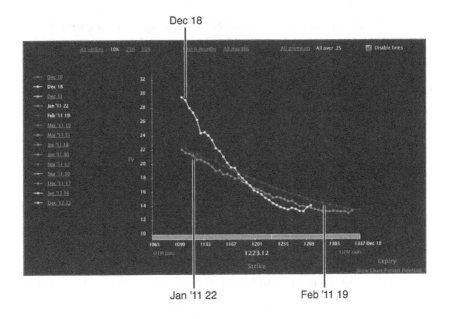

(Source: Livevol © www.livevol.com)

This type of understanding can help traders not only trade calendars, but double diagonals, butterflies, and condors as well.

Taking on the Skew

Mark Sebastian wrote the following in his OptionPit.com blog on 5/13/2010:

> The market continues to have a nice intraday and interday range. Even if it is going up and down to nowhere. With implied volatility at current levels, though, I think selling vol makes some sense. The problem for most traders is that they want to sell the ATM vol, which while the juiciest also is the most fairly priced. The skew, which still is somewhat elevated (although not to the level it was), is likely the better sale. The problem is it is hard to do this without getting long premium, but it can be done, in a few ways:
>
> 1. Ratio Spread. This is not a bad trade, except that if the market really falls out, the trader could lose on this one. If trading a ratio, I think the best money would be in buying an ATM put and selling OTM puts. At the same time, make sure to buy some extra protection on the way downside (that's right traders, units).
>
> 2. Condor/Strangle. I like the strangle better, but because of margin, traders might have to settle for condors. The key is to sell at the inflection point where the vega of the option really falls off. This way the trader can take the best advantage of the elevated implied volatility. Still, the trader has to buy volatility even lower and higher on the curve.
>
> 3. Finally, the most underutilized and possibly the best play for the money right now, in my opinion, is the double diagonal. I would be looking to sell the front money OTM call and put, and buy the back month OTM even further out. Here is one play I am looking at: May is done, it is all gamma, I would stay away. This leaves June, which, while not sky-high in the skew like May, is still very elevated in its puts and calls. July and August are elevated but not nearly the way that June is. Now I need to decide what strikes to trade. I am going to set up the trade vega positive, but after I

weight the vega, I should be negative. Here is one example in the OEX.

At first glance the spread has a vega of about 82. For the size of the position, I am going to call that pretty flat. However, once I weight the vega I find that I am short about 170.00 weighted vega.

Product Expiration	SPX Days	IV	Raw Vega	Multi- plier	Con- tracts	Line Weighted Vega
Based expiration	30					
June 550 C	37	17.3	51	0.900	-10	-459.229672
June 500 P	37	27	54	0.900	-10	-486.243182
July 570 C	65	16.3	50	0.679	10	339.6831102
July 480 P	65	29.2	64	0.679	10	434.7943811
Net weighted vega						-170.995363

This spread will make money if the skew flattens, if the spread between the June and July tightens, or even if IV in general falls relative to how it ran up. If a trader wants to trade the front month smile, without a huge outlay of capital (relative to a strangle), I think this is a decent trade.

Four Tips When the VIX Cash Is Depressed

Mark Sebastian wrote the following in his OptionPit.com blog on 3/23/2010:

It is all over the blogosphere that the VIX futures are far exceeding the cash VIX. "So what?" the trader may ask. "How is this of any use to me?" It is pretty simple: trading approach. When the VIX futures are far ahead of the VIX cash, it becomes visible in the options via the term risk. The front month is cheap relative to the back month. On the floor I would have tried to buy gamma and sell vega. A pretty easy task; all the trader has to do is sell time spreads. For the retail trader this process is a little harder. This is because most retail traders do not sit on a ton of margin. This does not mean that the trader needn't heed the VIX-Futures spread. Here are four things retail traders can do with options when the term spread is wide.

1. **Avoid long term-risk plays**—This means calendars, double diagonals, you name it. If a trader insists on putting on a calendar, try overlaying a little extra back month IV, or buying some cheap front month strangles against the position.

2. **Don't fear the front month**—Notice I didn't say, "Don't sell the front month." It can be okay to trade butterflies when IV is low, as long as the trader sets his or her wings using a standard deviation calculation. What I like to do is assume I will be in the trade for 18.5 days. Then set my wing width based on the ATM strike implied volatility. This will cause my wings to be wider in high IV months and tighter in low IV months. This is a great way to mitigate risk in the instance of a breakout of low IVs (post a comment or two if you traders would like a more detailed example; this might be a great topic for the next article).

3. **If the back month is still elevated over the front, then why fear the condor?**—The IV term structure of options is currently very similar to what it was in January. Traders, condors did FINE in that cycle. This is because condor traders were selling the month that was relatively high.

4. **As stated in number 1, don't be afraid to spend a little bit of cash on some cheap puts**—Nothing will cost so little and let the trader sleep so well. As my friend and Seven Time Broker of the Year Kevin Kennedy used to say: "Buy 'em when you can, not when you have to! Because when you have to buy them, you can't!!!"

How to Find and Track Volatility Skew

Mark Sebastian wrote the following in his OptionPit.com blog on 4/02/2009:

> *How does one find volatility skew?* Is this accomplished by studying the matrix with implied volatility and comparing daily IV? By finding richer condors? Every stock has volatility skew. Some will be steeper than others. ***The best way to track skew is by looking at the volatility of several options with a specific delta.*** You keep track of the skew by charting the changes in the volatility of these specific delta options and the spreads between them. For instance, one might want to keep track of the 5 delta put, the 20 delta put, the 50 delta call, the 25 delta call, and the 10 delta call. Why these options? I think using these options can give a fairly accurate representation of the skew curve. After picking your options, keep track of the volatility, but more importantly, the volatility spreads from strike to strike and option to option. Put them into Excel, and fill it in every day. Run a graph over the vols and you will really be able to see the skew curve. Run a second graph over the differences in the vol spread, and you will really be able to see how the curve is moving. Generally, when we get to about 15 days to expiration, I like to switch to the next month out. Here's a nice reminder to switch: ***When you hit the first of the month, you should no longer be using that month to chart skew.*** In your charts, make sure to note when you switch months. You will actually begin to notice patterns in how the skew curve moves. As far as condors, those are a good indicator that something is happening, and maybe a very quick shortcut. However, it's not a wonderful way to really track skew.

SPX Skew: It's All Relative

Mark's students constantly review how important the volatility surface is. They all know the difference between a high skew and a low skew. However, they sometimes fail to grasp one important factor: Skew is a percentage of ATM IV and only a relative number. ATM implied volatility matters. Here is an example:

You have two trades you could enter:

Trade 1: SPX iron condor sold at 15 delta

Downside skew is somewhat steep—the ten delta put trades at 140% of ATM IV.

ATM IV is 19%, and median IV of the stock is 23%.

Upside call skew is flat, and 25 delta call is trading at 90% of ATM IV.

Trade 2: SPX iron condor sold at 15 delta

Downside skew is somewhat normal—the ten delta put trades at 135% of ATM IV.

ATM IV is 25%, and median IV of the stock is 23%.

Upside call skew is normal, and 25 delta call is trading at 85% of ATM IV.

Conclusion:

Which trade is better? Note that 140% of 19 is IV of **26.6%,** whereas 135% of 25 is **33.75%.** On the call end of the trade, 85% of 25 is **21.25%,** whereas 90% of 19 is **17.1%.** Even though the skew is low, the fact that the IV itself was somewhat elevated makes a big difference.

The Point:

Volumes go up and down. The lower the volume, the more you need skew to make up for it. The higher the volume, the less skew matters, although a combo of high skew and high ATM IV is the best setup.

Understanding Implied Volatility in Iron Condors

Mark had an interesting discussion with one of his option mentoring students. He was in the middle of commenting on how he did not like the way iron condors looked at the moment. Mark had good reasons:

- Implied volatility was relatively low in terms of where it had been over the last few months (not in terms of realized volatility).

- Put skew was flat not just in December, but also in January.

- There was not a big volatility premium in selling the December or January relative front month volatility or realized volatility.

The option mentoring student responded by saying that he could still get .60 when he sold his short put and calls ten points wide at the 10 delta strike. Didn't that mean that the trade was still okay? No. Examine the put side of an SPX iron condor sold 36 days out at the 10 delta strike, as shown in Figure 11.1.

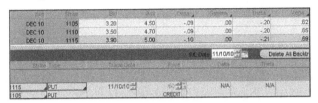

	Strike	Bid	Ask	Delta	Gamma	Theta	Vega
DEC 10	1105	3.20	4.50	-.09	.00	-.20	.62
DEC 10	1110	3.50	4.70	-.09	.00	-.20	.65
DEC 10	1115	3.90	5.00	-.10	.00	-.21	.69

P/L Date 11/10/10 — Delete All Backtr

Strike	Type	Trade Date	Price	Delta	Theta
1115	PUT	11/10/10	.60 CREDIT	N/A	N/A
1105	PUT				

Figure 11.1 SPX 1115/1105 DEC 10 put spread information. (Source: TD Ameritrade, Inc. Used with permission. For illustrative purposes only. TD Ameritrade, Inc., and Option Pit LLC are separate unaffiliated companies and are not responsible for each other's services or policies.)

SPX trades at 1218 and the trade collects .60. It places at the 1115/1105 strike, about 8.5% out-of-the-money.

Look at the condor only one month prior, as shown in Figure 11.2.

Strikes: ALL		PUTS				
Exp	Strike	Bid	Ask	Delta	Gamma	Theta	Vega
NOV 10	1045	3.10	4.20	-.08	.00	-.20	.57
NOV 10	1050	3.30	4.30	-.09	.00	-.20	.59
NOV 10	1055	3.70	4.90	-.10	.00	-.22	.64

P/L Date 10/12/10 — Delete All Backtr

Strike	Type	Trade Date	Price	Delta	Theta
1055	PUT	10/12/10	.60 CREDIT	1.31	1.77
1045	PUT				

Figure 11.2 SPX 1055/1045 NOV 10 put spread information. (Source: TD Ameritrade, Inc. Used with permission. For illustrative purposes only.)

With SPX closing at just under 1170, you sold the 1055/1045 spread and collected the same .60. However, the 1055s were not 8.5% out-of-the-money; they were just under 10% out-of-the-money. In absolute terms the spread is an extra 15 points wide on the downside. The same would hold true if you did the upside of the spread as well (although the two would likely be a smaller difference in absolute terms).

All credits are not created equal. Just because you collect .60 from a 10 delta spread doesn't mean it's a good trade. Volatility and volatility skew will pull in the wings of an iron condor. Unlike a butterfly, in which this can mitigate risk, this makes the iron condor more vulnerable to trouble in the event that implied volatility blows up.

The Stages of Skew

Mark Sebastian wrote the following in his OptionPit.com blog on 8/29/2011:

> A student asked me why the SPX had such a steep volatility skew (sometimes called smile) in September and October. The VIX was coming in; shouldn't skew flatten as implied volatilities drop? SPX skew is steep, more so in October than in September (although it's elevated there too), where the 10 delta put is trading at a volatility of about 152% of the ATM straddle.
>
> While it's clear that IV is coming down and fear has subsided substantially in the short term with the Fed meeting over and [Hurricane] Irene passing, we are certainly not in a stage of calm either. A VIX of over 32 is historically astronomically high, as it is more than 50% elevated relative to the long-term mean of the VIX. One thing to remember is when IV is coming in, the market typically will want to keep bidding up those baby puts for a long time, because of overall fear of IV going higher instead of back toward the mean. This brings us to the 5 major phases of volatility skew:

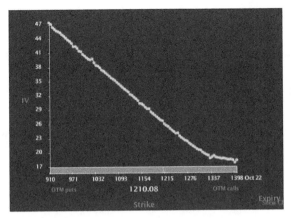

(Source: Livevol © www.livevol.com)

Phase 1: Calm

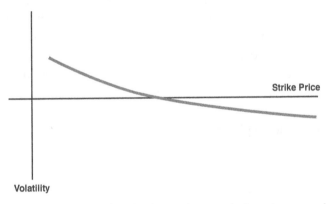

In this phase, implied volatility is low and skew is normal to flattish. This phase is what we would call "normal times," where the VIX is between 16% and 18%. The market may have ups and downs, but there is little fear of a "major event" or a multi-standard deviation outlier day.

Phase 2: Calm Before the Storm

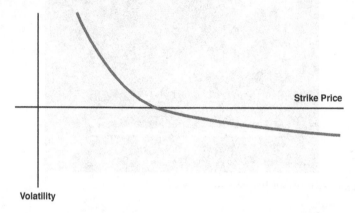

In this phase, IV is still somewhat low, but may be slightly elevated or not 15-20 in the VIX. However, there is some developing fear of a major standard deviation event. It can also occur when IV is "oversold" and there is some pent-up selling. This phase can lead to the next phase or right back to calm (Phases 2 and 4 can move in either direction). Basically, the market is starting to buy protection, but doesn't want to own ATM options, thus buying of "unit puts" pushes up skew.

Phase 3: The Typhoon

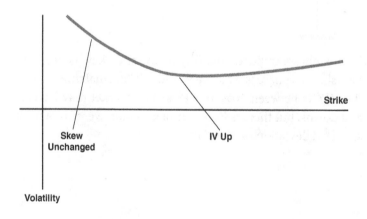

In this phase, there is extreme fear in the market and the VIX is at 30% to 40% or greater. We were just in this phase as late as last week. IV on the downside of the curve is still high, but ATM IV is up so much that skew actually flattens. This is a condition of borderline panic.

Phase 4: The Calming Storm

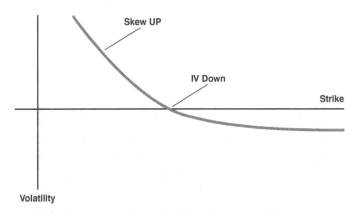

IV is still quite high in this phase, but it is falling. The market thinks things might be getting better but is afraid that things could get bad again. ATM IV is being sold off, but many of those selling ATM volatility are buying out-of-the-money puts. Unit protection is at its most expensive in this phase, as ATM IV is elevated and skew is steep. The VIX can be anywhere from 20% to 35% in this phase. Like Phase 2, the Calming Storm can blow up into a Typhoon again, or it can move toward Phase 5.

Phase 5

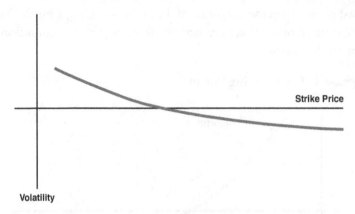

All is well, in this phase, as IV returns to normal, but skew stays slightly elevated for a period of time as the market licks its wounds from recent losses. The only difference between this phase and Phase 1 is that skew might be slightly steeper, and IV may move a little more quickly off of lows. This phase can jump to Phase 1 or Phase 2. It can take up to 6 months for Phase 5 to turn into a fully calm situation.

In between the 5 main phases there are many small phases and transitions, but I thought it might interest you traders who watch skew to see a clear example of how skew can go from calm to crazy to calm.

12

Lessons from the Trading Floor on Risk Management

Cash Is a Position

Cash is a position you can take. Being in cash has some serious advantages, yet many are afraid of the position. Table 12.1 shows two annual returns in which $10,000 traded in iron condors.

Table 12.1 Two Scenarios for Iron Condor Returns

	Set 1	Set 2
Jan	$ 700	$ 700
Feb	$ 200	$ 200
Mar	$ (1,100)	$ (1,100)
Apr	$ 500	$ 500
May	$ 300	$ 300
Jun	$ (700)	$ (700)
Jul	$ 300	$ 300
Aug	$ 400	$ 400
Sep	$ (600)	$ -
Oct	$ 800	$ 800
Nov	$ 200	$ 200
Dec	$ (300)	$ (300)
Total	**$ 700**	**$ 1,300**

The net simple return on the data set was $700 or 7%, not bad at all.

Now examine this second data set. The net simple return on the data set was $1,300 or 13%, almost *double*.

The only difference between the two sets was in September. You decided to stay in cash. Believe it or not, you made more money not trading. You might know this urge to trade, this need or want. It should be resisted when you don't see anything that you like. If you do not like what you see, skip trading and drink a Diet Coke. You will be far more relaxed and will likely have more money. It may not be sexy, but in the end I'd rather be rich than sexy.

Better yet, there is an old saying that there is always something worth trading. If you do not like what you see, start expanding your knowledge base so that you can recognize opportunities. It can make a huge difference in your trading life.

The Card Game Value

One of the most loved trades by the retail public is the "credit spread." One of the biggest mistakes the retail public makes is failing to exit credit spreads when the short option becomes inexpensive. This is not because they want to hold the trade to expiration. It is because most do not understand that there is a second component in the value of options that most option pricing models cannot calculate. This component will cause the final portion of the value of an option to take much longer to decay than the model predicts. This value exists because of the payout disparity if the option goes sour (unit risk). This is *The Card Game Value.*

Understanding this allows you to exit trades at an earlier date and move money into trades that follow the standard option model.

The Card Game: Two men are going to play a card game; they will play it only once. There are 100 cards. Ninety-nine of the cards have a value of 0 and one card has a value of 1,000. One of the men will pay the other for the chance to draw one card. If he draws the 0, he gets nothing; if he draws the 1,000, the other man must pay him $1,000. Theoretically, the card game is worth $10 (1,000×1/100). But what do you think the one man should charge the other to play the game? If this game were played over and over, the man would probably charge a very low number, say $11. He would know that over time probabilities are in his favor and he will come out ahead (this is how Las Vegas pays for all those nice hotels). However, this game will be played only once. The odds are the same, but if the $1000 card is drawn, the man on the hook will have no opportunity to make the money back. My guess is that it would take a lot more than $11 to get someone to play this game.

This thought process is exactly what throws off the value of cheap options. The probabilities say that the option should be worth nothing, but the option will maintain a value of .10 to .25 for an exceptionally long time. That is because the person who sells the cheap option is the same as the man who is selling the draw in our card game. The person would make money over time in a Vegas world, but option months have a limited life. If the seller of the cheap option has the trade go bad, he will never see that money again. The trader will not have an unlimited number of chances to play this game. The major move has happened; the trader has lost. To make matters worse, unlike in the card game, the trader has an undefined risk, meaning that he has no idea how much he will lose if the trade goes against him.

The final 0.25 of an option takes much longer to decay out. What does this mean to you as a credit spread trader? Take off credit spreads when they no longer follow the model and only have *Card Game Value*. This improves your performance because you free up capital earlier to move into other trades, which pricing models and Greeks can value, and can be out of your trades earlier (always a good thing). Credit spreads are a great way to make money, but it takes only one bad draw to wipe you out. Don't get caught *playing cards*.

Why Are Option Trading Hands So Hard to Sit On?

Mark Sebastian wrote the following in his OptionPit.com blog on 12/28/2010:

> Once I have been working with an options mentoring student for a little while, they can usually figure out how to properly set up a trade. That is about half of the battle; the next step is managing and adjusting. This is where I can run into problems. Most of my students get the way to adjust, and can even understand the when; it's the when not to that seems to kill them. Here is a DIA position that we are currently working on in the AM Pit Report:

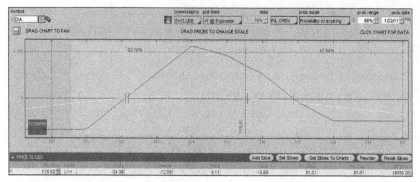

(Source: TD Ameritrade, Inc. Used with permission. For illustrative purposes only.)

Looking at the position, does it need adjusting? If so, what should I do to fix this position?

If your answer was anything besides NO and NOTHING, you may have a case of over-adjusting disease. I am not sure why people get this disease but it is rampant in the trading world. The main symptom is that a trader makes trades in a position that is not in trouble but is near a point where the position might start to get into trouble. This disease kills more trades than the market, and here is why.

Every time you make an adjustment on a position, it puts the trader in the trade longer and costs the trader commissions. The longer one is in a trade, the longer one is likely to get a major multi-standard deviation move. It is the big huge moves that kill a trade, not the slow creeps up or down. We can adjust a position to small ups and downs. The small moves can also turn around without us having to adjust; remember, just because a position is NEAR trouble doesn't mean it's going to get in trouble. Underlying securities do turn around or stop moving sometimes. On the other hand, multi-standard deviation moves will likely hurt any trade even if it is adjusted. You can protect a position from a lot of moves, but not all.

So how can I tell if I should adjust a position? That is hard to say. However, here is a test I like to use: Push your current position forward 3 days, then look at the position. Ask yourself, If I do nothing, am I likely to make money/break even if we stay here, rally a standard deviation, or fall a standard deviation? If the answer is yes to at least 2 out of 3 of those, do nothing, if it is not, then consider looking at adjusting.

Trading isn't an easy job; the last thing traders should be doing is making it more difficult by adding commission and time to their income trade.

How Option Time Value Premium Decays over the Weekend

The following is from Mark Sebastian's Option Pit Blog on 10/29/2009 (at the time it was called Option911):

A retail trader had on a calendar spread (long time spread) that was going very well. On a Friday, his calendar position was up 18%. He was excited because if he could just hold on through the weekend, he was going to collect another 4% return on his capital.

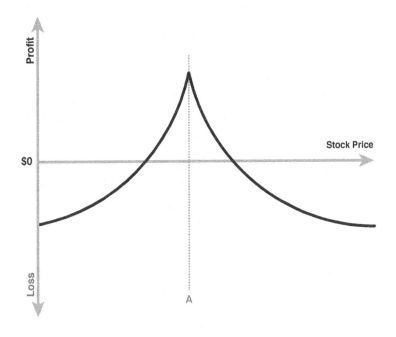

On Monday he was quite despondent. He had held his position over the weekend, and after the market movement that Monday morning, he was down from Friday. The student said, "Mark, I don't get it. I did my analysis. I should be up at least a few hundred dollars from last Friday. How come I didn't make anything over the weekend?"

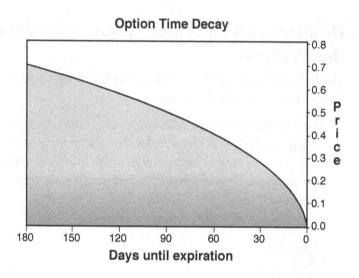

Option Time Decay

Here is the short answer: Weekend theta is decayed out of a position by Friday afternoon at 4:00 p.m. Most retail traders assume that theta decay is linear. Over time, theta decays at the rate that your trade software says it does.

For instance, if certain trading software said a position had a positive decay of 10, most retail traders would assume they would have an extra 10 dollars by the following trading morning. But what about the weekend?

Market makers are not stupid (well, some are). They don't like giving away free money. If the position didn't decay out before Friday's close, other traders would come in, sell a large amount of premium at the end of the day on Friday, and then buy to close first thing on Monday morning. Traders who sold the premium would be happy. They would have gotten the entire weekend's decay, 2 1/2 days (Friday 4 p.m. to Monday 9:30 a.m.), for the price of one wake-up (Sunday 4:00 p.m. till Monday morning).

So what do market makers do? It's pretty simple. We begin to decay the entire weekend as early as possible. Although every market maker manages weekend decay differently, Mark might have done this: On Thursday about midday Mark would turn off all of his quotes. He would go into his options quoting software and begin moving his software's theoretical day forward Friday (this is very similar to using the date function in TOS, OV, or Trade Station).

Mark would notice that other traders began selling premium. He would not want to buy premium that would decay for two days while the market is closed. So he had two choices. He could lower the theoretical volatility. This would reduce his option prices based on premium sellers' activity. Or he could move the theoretical date forward. This would reduce the theoretical value of the options using days to expiration instead of lowering the implied volatility (this is the one time where the days to expiration portion of the five functions of a pricing model can matter as much as volatility).

On Friday morning, Mark would already have the theoretical date to set Saturday's date. This let him stay ahead of the game. Once he saw premium sellers acting, he would move the theoretical date forward to Sunday. At the close of the day on Friday, Mark would have his system set to 4 p.m. EST on Sunday.

The system would have one wake-up (Sunday 4 p.m. to Monday 9:30 a.m.) of theoretical decay left priced into the options he traded. There was no "free" premium. So how does this knowledge affect you as a retail options trader? You may note that current software does not take weekend decay into account.

You, as a savvy option trader, can. If you are in an option trade on the cusp of exit on a Friday afternoon, get out of the position. There is not 2 1/2 days of premium to be made over the weekend, and you have already made a chunk of theta. A few people may think that they can make money by buying premium; this is also not the case because you still have to pay the wake-up decay (Sunday at 4 p.m. till Monday at 9:30 a.m.). There is no "weekend edge." There is only the trader's edge—your ability to perform better than other traders.

When Is the Time to De-risk Your Portfolio?

The term "de-risk" means to execute an activity or a series of activities to lower the risks to your portfolio. For most people de-risking a portfolio means reducing positions, which in turn reduces exposure.

So when should you take off risk? In these situations:

- The portfolio is so volatile that you can't sleep at night.
- The market environment has changed and you don't have a read on the new environment.
- You have hit your portfolio trading loss limits.
- Your trading model is not working in the current market environment.
- You need to rebalance the portfolio.
- Your positions have hit their target profits.

De-risking is a very important part of successfully managing TOMIC. Make sure you know when to pull the parachute chord. Don't hesitate in pulling it. It is better to be safe than sorry.

How to Trade When You Go on Vacation

How a trader should trade when going on vacation is simple: Go flat. Don't leave trades on. If you do, they should be long-term. Assume that you won't have access to the Internet, and that your traveling partner will not be happy with you if you are constantly checking your account. It is no fun to be on vacation and trade at the same time. That is why it is called a vacation.

You might find yourself on a cruise ship claiming to have Internet available. However, when you are cruising in Alaska in the middle of glacier territory, that Internet connection does not work. You might be unable to check your account for several days. Be fully engaged when you are managing your portfolio, but let go when you are on vacation. If you don't have the luxury of going flat when you go on vacation, you should get a trading partner to take care of the portfolio while you are away.

13

Lessons from the Trading Floor on Trading and Execution

What Everybody Should Know About Payment for Order Flow

ark Sebastian wrote the following in his OptionPit.com blog on 12/20/2009:

When I first began trading in 2001, a market making firm, let's call it Firm XYZ, came up with a new and innovative idea to bring option volume to the Pits where they controlled the most volume, the Pits where they were the Specialist, or the Designated Primary Market-Maker or DPM.

This was called **payment for order flow.** The exchanges call them "marketing fees" and your broker may call it one of many names.

What seemed like a bright idea at the time has blossomed into a situation that is

- Bad for the customer

- Bad for the liquidity provider

- GREAT for your online broker

In the following years, the system would slowly become integrated by the exchanges and taken out of the individual firm's hands. The system has essentially morphed into a hierarchy that *puts trading firms who are willing to pay to see larger orders in the driver's seat, and the public in the trunk.* I will not broach the hierarchy subject for large orders, but I will explain why it is important that one takes the time to review the status of their order.

GETTING THE FIRST LOOK

Back to Firm XYZ, the well-meaning market making firm that opened Pandora's box. (I will be picking on Firm XYZ during this article, but this is industry practice. I do not want the reader to think they are the only firm that does this. As stated above, most EXCHANGES now engage in this practice.) They made agreements with many trading firms to get a "first look" at all of the paper that a certain firm has. But what does that "first look" really mean?

- If Firm XYZ is matching the NBBO, and the order is hitting the NBBO, the order will route to Firm XYZ's pit.

- If Firm XYZ wasn't the best bid or offer, depending on the order, Firm XYZ might still get first look at the order. By routing through linkage, the order would get sent to the exchange with the best bid or offer.

- If Firm XYZ was matching the NBBO, and an order did not hit the NBBO, the order would still route to Firm XYZ. As a retail trader, one might look at that deal and think that it isn't so bad. That trader would be sorely mistaken.

The first part of the deal likely has little effect on retail traders as they are hitting the NBBO. Likely their order will get filled. The only time this would be a problem is if the trader is sending a large trade and the order is being sent to the exchange with the smallest bid or offer. It is possible that a small portion of the trader's order could get filled, and while being linked to another exchange the market changes on the trader. This would leave the trader open on a portion of his or her trade.

The second situation, where the market making firm isn't matching the NBBO, yet sees the order first, then routes the order through linkage, is slightly more problematic. If there is only one exchange bid at a certain level, the seconds it takes the order to move from the Firm XYZ through linkage to the exchange, a market can certainly move (actually I believe many firms that accept payment for order flow have some sort of matching guarantee to protect their customers from this occurrence).

Finally, the real culprit, a *non-marketable order gets sent to the market making pit.* The example I am about to run through actually happened to me in IBM.

Imagine that the ISE is willing to pay 50 cents for an option up to 5,000 times and the PHLX is willing to pay 50 cents up to 30 times. If a trader had an order to sell an option for 55 cents 10 times, would the trader expect it to be sent to the ISE or the PHLX? The trader would expect it to go to the ISE; the firm accepting Payment for Order Flow would send it to the PHLX. This is bad news for the trader because the order is being sent to a place with the fewest number of eyes on it. *This matters!!* I have seen offers sitting on the PHLX while that price is trading on the CBOE. As I have stated before, *the only thing smart about a smart router is that it is smart for your broker to make the most money.*

When Should You Worry About Assignment?

Mark Sebastian wrote the following in his OptionPit.com blog on 2/07/2010:

> I want to discuss something somewhat basic that seems to hound me constantly: **retail traders asking me if I am worried about being assigned on a short put position.** The very neophyte traders will sometimes go so far as to ask if I am worried about call assignment. I am going to give the short answer on assignment, and then I am going to prove it. Then I will discuss when it is okay to consider assignment. Very quickly, as traders being assigned should be one of the last things we worry about. The reason being, it isn't something that happens very often.

The circumstances when a trader will be assigned are actually somewhat rare. This is especially true now with interest rates so low. Here is why: I am going to start with this statement, and it was one of the first things I learned as a trader. A put is a call and a call is a put. Almost every trade pro traders make is converting calls to puts and vice versa. For instance, the protective put: If one charts the graph of a protective put (long put + long stock), what does the trader notice? It looks exactly like a call. The position has a limited loss, and unlimited upside.

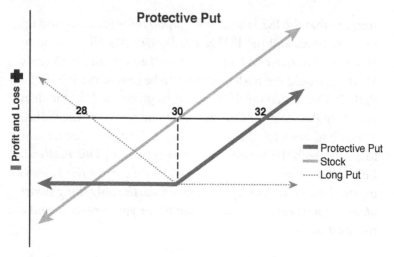

Another common trade, the covered call (long stock + short call) looks exactly like a short put. The position has a limited upside and an unlimited downside.

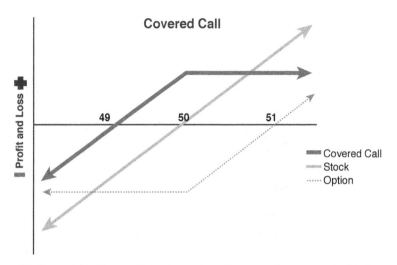

Covered Call

49   50   51

Profit and Loss

■ Covered Call
■ Stock
⋯ Option

If all combinations of stocks and options can be converted into other positions, then there must be some sort of force holding these combinations together. Similar to $E=MC^2$, the option world has a formula that holds it together called put-call parity. Put-call parity is the formula that ensures that traders cannot make more money buying calls than they can buying puts and stock. When options are out of parity, arbitrage begins; this quickly brings options back to parity. This Formula is Call–Put=Stock Price–Strike Price+(Interest–Dividends). The short equation is $C-P=S-X+(I-D)$; the I–D is often replaced with a K for cost of carry.

Using this formula, if a customer wants to sell the February 50 call at 9 dollars, with the stock trading 55.00 and a cost of carry of 0.20, what would the put be trading? $9-P=55-50+.20$. The put should be trading around 3.80. If the put had a bid of 4.00, the market makers would buy as many calls as they could for 9 dollars, sell the stock against the calls (converting them into puts), then sell the puts. This would allow them to synthetically buy the put and then sell the actual put.

Let's think about put-call parity and assignment. If I am long a put, and long the underlying against that put, what position do I really have? I am long a call. If I really have on a call, then the only way I would exercise my put was if the value of the call was less than the value of the put, stock, and cost of carry combination or C.

If I had bought an ATM butterfly in OEX on January 19th, I may have entered into the OEX 500/530/560 put fly. On February 5th, the OEX is 40 points lower trading at 491.35; the 530 puts are trading 41.50. With a market maker interest rate of .25 and a cash accrued dividend of about $2.95, our cost of carry ends up being about -2.90. The calls are trading .15 cents. Would I exercise the puts? Is .15<491.35–530+(–2.90)+41.5?

491.35–530+(–2.90)+41.5=–.05. The answer is *no*; thus despite a *major* down swing, it is not in my counterparties' best interest to exercise the put. With interest rates this low, assignments are few and far between. The Market Maker rate will have to increase by at least 1% before this position becomes a somewhat attractive exercise candidate, even with an 8% down move.

Hopefully by now one can see there are few scenarios where the put should get assigned to seller. Calls are a slightly different story; nondividend paying calls should *never* be early exercised. However, traders are at risk of assignment if the underlying pays a dividend. Take EXC for instance: On February 11th, EXC goes ex-dividend paying 52.5 cents per share. If I am short the 40 calls, should I worry about getting assigned? I can figure it out by plugging the numbers into put call parity. The call is trading around 4.25, the put around .05. The stock is trading 44.25 and the cost of carry ends up being (.01–.525). Plugging these numbers, 4.25–.05=44.25–40+(.01+.525), the 40 calls have a problem; the C–P does not equal the S–X+K. Those calls will likely get assigned to me.

Now that we have run through the math, traders should certainly be clear about how to tell if they will be assigned, using slow long hand. I will give you what I am calling the "Traders Short Hand" to figure out assignment:

1. If the (i–d) is greater than the value of the call opposite the trader's short put, the trader may get assigned on the position. Generally, I do not pay attention to this until the call is worth less than .25 or so. With rates as low as they are, it is closer to .05.

2. If the dividend is greater than the value of the put opposite the trader's short call position, the trader is likely to get assigned on his or her short call position. If the call does not have a dividend, traders should never be assigned on the short position.

Traders have many risks associated with a position. It is important to concentrate on the most important risks, while ignoring the insignificant risks. In almost every case, save dividends, assignment risk is at or near the bottom of traders' risks.

A Successful Short SPX Calendar

Mark Sebastian reviewed an example of a short calendar trade in his blog entry of 8/24/10:

> Yesterday during the Mid-Day Pit Report I was pointing out how wide the IV spread was between September and October. With the market up on the day I pointed out that the implied volatility spread between the at-the-money September calls and the at-the-money October calls was almost 2 points. This drove the price over 14.00 at one point yesterday.

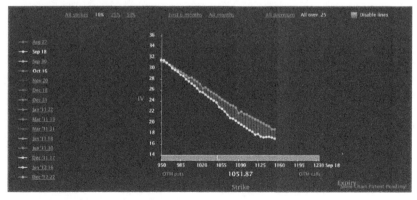

(Source: Livevol © www.livevol.com)

This trader did not get the best execution, but I wanted to relay the actual trade. The trade sold the Sep-Oct 1085 call spread with the SPX around 1080 for a credit of 13.25.

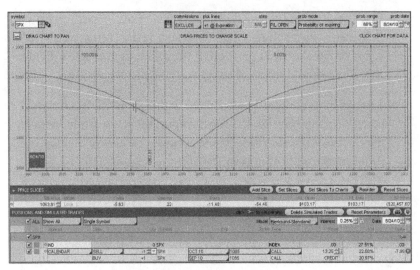

(Source: TD Ameritrade, Inc. Used with permission. For illustrative purposes only.)

That volatility spread was still over 1.5 points on this time spread. The trader then put in a bid to buy the spread back for 12.20. This would have been a return of 8% on a standard long calendar. However, the fill on the open this morning was good and it traded at 11.75. That is a return of 150.00 in a day, or 11.3%. This is in a single DAY.

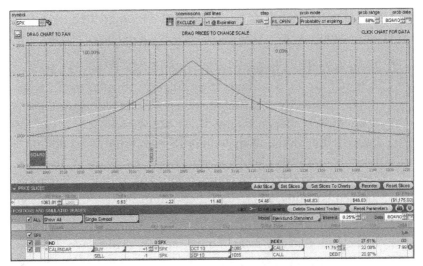

(Source: TD Ameritrade, Inc. Used with permission. For illustrative purposes only.)

This layup of a trade is no longer there, but will likely reappear to traders who understand how options function. Traders, this is the power of understanding volatility and term structure. Yes, it is very important to understand how to sell premium. But for any trader there is a lot more to learn than simply "sell a condor." One thing to remember, the other side of this calendar has lost what my trader has made. That is why we do not simply slap the same trade on every month.

Butterfly Trading Checklist

Mark Sebastian wrote the following in his OptionPit.com blog on 9/13/2010:

> Option mentoring is not an easy business. We are always look-ing for easy, simple answers to very complicated questions. One subject that one should really concentrate on is trade selection. There are mentors out there who suggest that the same trade every month works; these people are probably not trading. They say trade the same trade every month because it is simple. Trad-ing is not simple, trading is hard. However, we want to help. Thus, we developed a three-part checklist to tell whether it is

safe to enter a butterfly trade. There is a lot more to the success of a fly than these three things, but this is a good place to start.

1. Make sure that a trader pays attention to the IV of the butterfly. Believe it or not, the trader does not want to enter the fly when implied volatility is sky-high. When IVs are sky-high, there is likely to be a snapback rally. If IVs are too low, that is bad too because the trade is likely to have IV pop. I find that middle-of-the-road implied volatility is actually the best place to enter butterflies. If the IVs are in between 25%-75% of the 90-day mean implied volatility, feel free to check number one off. If too high or too low, no check box.

2. Make sure that the inter-month skew isn't too wide. If inter-month skew is too wide, this is another warning sign of a break-out. When inter-month skew is too negative, it can mean that in relative terms the front month is too high. Butterflies are a front month trade, thus we want to avoid this problem. If the skew is too positive, that likely means the market is moving around a lot in relative terms. Considering that butterflies are a gamma trade, this is also bad news. There are some really great ways to track this skew; one quick way is to compare VIX to VXV. This can give a pretty good idea of how 30-day volatility is behaving relative to 90-day vol. If the term spread is not too high or too low, put a check in the box; otherwise, we are a no go.

While 90-day vol is usually higher than 30-day vol, I think traders can see how points of widening coincide with major moves:

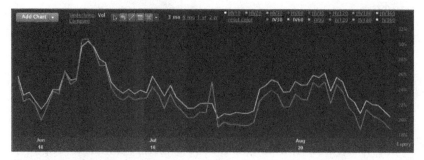

(Source: Livevol © www.livevol.com)

3. Watch Intra-Month skew. When skew is high, butterflies are a very tough trade (see May, June, and July for details). When skew is low, butterflies are an easy trade and cheap to ensure (see August).

What does this skew look like? Let's take a look.

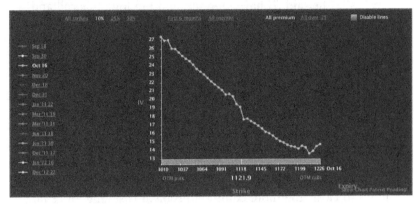

(Source: Livevol © www.livevol.com)

Again, this is not the answer to all trading questions. We did not attach any numeric guidelines, as should be done, for check boxes 2 and 3. Also, there are more things to look at than just these three. But this is a starting point. That said, if all three of these can be checked off, the butterfly is probably a favorable trade to enter at that given time. In this example, we don't think we can check off any of these three items.

What Is the Proper Width for an Index Butterfly's Wings?

Mark Sebastian wrote the following in his OptionPit.com blog on 11/29/2009:

> I was recently mentoring a student who had a split strike butterfly in MNX, or so he thought. I looked at the trade for a second; I quickly noticed that his wings were spaced REALLY wide.

I calmly spoke: "This is not a butterfly, *this is an unhedged strangle.*"

The student was flabbergasted. (BTW, is there a cooler word than *flabbergasted*? I think I have loved the word ever since Don Music wrote a song about the word on Sesame Street.)

"WHAT!" he said. "I have long see, and I'm long this call and this put!"

"Yes," I stated, "but those aren't a hedge against this position. Those options will have no effect on profit and loss. When you bought those options, you hedged NOTHING!"

The above conversation was not the first I've had concerning wing placement, nor will it be the last. Most traders can figure out which options they want to sell. *It's the options to buy that can turn into a big nightmare.* While some students set their longs to close, the more common problem is setting longs far too distant from the at-the-money strikes.

The purpose of the long options in a spread is to reduce margin, reduce the risk of the position, and maximize efficiency of capital. If a trader sets up a butterfly where *the longs do not significantly reduce the margin of the trade,* it is a *warning sign* that the *trade has wings too distant from the at-the-money strikes. When a butterfly's risk is significantly greater than the reward,* this is another *warning sign* that the *long options are too far from at the money.* If the underlying can move one standard deviation without having a significant impact on the price of the long, the wing is set out too far. This is a big problem because it can not only put too much capital at risk; it can mess with the trader's calculated return on capital. This can trick the trader into staying in a trade too long, open up the trader to substantial unnecessary loss, or both.

With these in mind, here are some guidelines traders can follow to set up butterfly wings:

1. *Options that are worth less than $0.25 do not hedge anything.*

   If a trader is setting up a butterfly that has him or her buying a wing under .25, the trader should not buy that option for a hedge (note I am not talking about units which are to be used as black swan insurance; this is a case in which the option is actually a part of the spread being entered). Here is why: If I buy a call option for .25 as a part of a butterfly, the underlying rallies three dollars, my short calls are probably losing a significant amount of money, my long strike that I bought for .25 is probably still worth about .25. Traders will find that buying options worth more than .25 when setting up trades will perform better and actually cost less.

2. *Look for at least a one-to-one risk reward.*

   If the trader sets up a butterfly where the risk is more than the maximum potential profit, the trader can likely reduce the margin easily at little or no cost to the trade.

3. *Always check the next closest strike.*

   When setting up a trade, if a trader can push the call down a strike, or the put up one strike and it costs the trade less than one to five margin to profit potential, it is probably worth strikes in. For instance, if a trader can make a one lot butterfly's wings five points closer and it costs the trader less than one hundred dollars, the trader likely has his long wings set too far from his short strikes.

4. If a trader sets up longs properly, **when that decay gets down to under $0.25**, the trader should consider either pulling out of the trade and taking his or her money, or kicking the wings in to reduce the margin on the trade.

Traders who keep these guidelines in mind when trading will find that they are using their capital more efficiently, putting less at risk, and most likely making more money.

The Importance of Good Exits

Having the right conditions before entering a trade is probably the most important factor in order to consistently make money. However, exiting a trade is the second-most-important condition. In fact, it is probably the most important condition in order to not lose much money. It is like having a balanced football team, a good offense and a good defense. The good trading offense is knowing your entry points. That means placing trades when conditions are in your favor and you have an edge. The good trading defense is knowing when to exit. That means closing a trade when you have won enough or before you lose too much.

When you board an airplane, the first thing the flight attendants point out is the emergency exits. This knowledge of the position of the emergency exits may save your life someday. In trading options for TOMIC, you need to know what your exit conditions are for the trades. When things start to go wrong, and when they do they go very quickly, you need to know where the emergency exit is.

At TOMIC, before you enter a trade, you need to know exactly when to exit. There are always at least two exit points for a trade:

1. The exit when the trade is going against you.

2. The exit when the trade is going in your favor.

When the trade is going against you, when it is not working out, you should exit without hesitation. Like that emergency exit, it must be used. This prevents major losses in the portfolio. You might hesitate in taking the exit because you don't want the loss. You could believe that the market could change direction in the next minutes or hours and things will improve. This thinking might or might not work. But if you are not disciplined, a small loss could become a giant loss. That giant loss might be unrecoverable. This is the same thinking that makes gamblers go broke. The losing gamblers keep playing until they lose all their money because they always think that their luck must turn around in the next bet. Taking the loss at a predetermined point helps control this impulse and limits the losses. The best loss is the first loss.

When a trade is going in your favor, you need to know when to exit the trade and take profits. You might keep the trade on because you think that there are more profits to be made, when suddenly the market reverses and wipes out the entire profit. Consider using a percentage of margin as the parameter to trigger the exit.

Here is an example. When entering an iron condor trade, you might set the exit at a loss of 20% of margin or at a gain of 15% of margin. If the trade goes against you, you might make adjustments to try to manage the deltas. However, when the trade hits a loss of 20%, you need to exit. The same holds if the trade hits a profit of 15%.

There are variations on this. Some traders managing large positions might decide to exit using scales. So if a trade is going in your favor, instead of waiting for the 15% gain, you might sell part of the position gaining 10%, and then sell another part, gaining 15%. The exit points are just examples. In real life you should define your own exit parameters, but it is imperative before entering the trade. Be disciplined and follow your predefined exit criteria. Having predefined exits for your trades saves you money and makes your trades more profitable.

Preparing to Trade for a Living, How Much Capital Is Needed?

To trade for a living as a professional, you need to be prepared. You need knowledge, mental discipline, and financial means.

People who trade for a living are those who trade on their own hook. They are the masters of their own destinies. They report to themselves, and they know whether they are winning or losing in the game of trading by looking at the balance in their trading accounts.

Before you begin to trade for a living, you need to know your annual expenses. How much do you need to live on? Then make sure you have at least two years' worth of savings. So if your annual living expenses are $60,000, you should have $120,000 saved liquid. Next, you need to know the returns you have been averaging on your part-time trades. Before you embark on trading for a living, you need to first experience trading. So if you have been averaging a 2% profit (return on Reg-T margin) per month over the past two years, you have more than 500 trades under your belt. Hence, if you average 2% per month, you are able to produce 24% return per year, assuming that you are fully invested all the time. In reality, you probably won't have all your capital invested. Most likely you will have between 40% and 60% on a normal basis. On average, assume you will be 50% invested. Now, do the math to figure out how much money you will need to have before starting your trading-for-a-living venture.

Here is the calculation to start your venture. First, you will need enough savings to cover two years' worth of living expenses, which is $120,000. Next, you need enough investment capital to earn enough to cover your living expenses. So if you can consistently earn 2% per month on each trade and you need $60,000 per year or $5,000 a month, you will need $5,000/0.02= $250,000. But wait—if you are investing on average only 50% of your capital, then you will need $500,000 of investment capital.

So to start to trade for a living, you need to have $120,000 (savings) + $500,000 (working capital) = $620,000. Be prepared psychologically to run your option trading as a business, like TOMIC. If in two years you have been able to cover your expenses and increase your savings, you are doing very well. If in two years you have earned your living and maintained your savings at the same level at which you started, you are doing well. However, if in two years you have depleted your savings and have not been able to cover your expenses by trading, consider the possibility that trading for a living is not for you. If this is the case and you still wish to continue, hire a coach and reread this book!

The Importance of Focus

Have you ever...

- Felt overwhelmed by too much information?
- Wanted to trade every market that a talking head on TV recommended?
- Traded multiple markets with different strategies at the same time? And lost on every trade?
- Frozen like a deer in the headlights during a flash crash?
- Analyzed a trade over and over again without placing it, only to place it when the trade had already played out?

- Felt like switching strategies every day?

- Bought a new investment newsletter every time you got an e-mail about how great the newsletter was?

- Wanted to change professions after the market moved against you?

- Traded when you were upset, and made a lot of costly mistakes?

- Lost money when trading after a close friend or relative died?

If you answered yes to any of these questions, you might have problems focusing. Being able to focus is a key ability to be successful as a manager of TOMIC or in any other endeavor.

When a surgeon operates, he has to concentrate on doing everything correctly to save the patient's life. He must not be thinking about his dinner date with his new girlfriend. He should be focused on getting the surgery done successfully. Would you be comfortable going into an eye surgery when your doctor tells you that his mother just died, but not to worry because he can do your surgery in his sleep? Of course not.

The same applies to the person running TOMIC. You have to be focused on what you are doing when you are trading. If you are running TOMIC, you are running a business. The well-being of the shareholders (you and your investors) depends on your decisions.

When Michael Jordan had the ball with only a couple of seconds left in the game, what was he thinking? Did he hear the crowd cheering? Did he listen to the opponent players' trash talk? No, he was in the zone; he was totally focused on one thing and one thing only: scoring to win the game. When you are managing TOMIC, your focus must be like a laser. You need to be alert and maintain your discipline in order to manage risks and book profits.

Steve Jobs, Apple Computer's innovator, was very good at what he did. He focused on creating elegant and simple devices for the consumer. Because of his focus, he was able to reveal the needs that people didn't know they had and that technology could solve. The many uses of the iPad were not imagined by consumers until they had an iPad.

Daniel (Ralph Macchio), in the movie *Karate Kid II* (1986), was able to break six slabs of ice with one knife-hand strike because he was able to focus and concentrate all the force of his body into one small area of impact.

What does all this mean to you, as TOMIC manager? It means that you need to define who you are. Know your investment strategy and how you are going to implement it. Once you do, don't get sidetracked by other investors, markets, strategies, or products. Stay focused on what you are doing.

14

Lessons from the Trading Floor on the Other Greeks

What Happens to the Gamma of ITM or OTM Options When IV Increases?

ark Sebastian wrote the following in his OptionPit.com blog on 12/29/2010:

When I am working with option mentoring students, for the most part they can figure out at-the-money options. They get that as the strike becomes more ATM, the delta change from 50 delta to the next strike in either direction has decreased because of volatility. But what about out-of-the-money options? Do out-of-the-money options lose gamma, or gain with an increase in IV? The answer is both!

For options that are well out of the money (below a 15 delta), in general any increase in implied volatility is going to increase gamma. This is very significant for condor and strangle traders to understand. They need to know that initially, when the IV increases on their condor, the condor is going to have more delta sensitivity in a downturn than the model predicts. Take a look; here is an MNX condor with strikes that are 10% out of the money.

▼ PRICE SLICES						Add Slice	Set Slices	Set Slices To Charts	Reorder	Reset Slices
221.00	-10%	-51.96	-2.80	7.52	-36.68	($480.59)	($480.59)	($4,900.59)		
200.91	Live	2.01	-2.35	7.31	-30.36	$6.66	$6.66	($4,011.55)		
180.82	-10%	45.68	-2.19	7.56	-27.35	($475.80)	($475.80)	($4,092.20)		

POSITIONS AND SIMULATED TRADES							Delete Simulated Trades	Reset Parameters		
☑ ALL Show All	Single Symbol					Model Bjerksund-Stensland	Interest 0.25%	Date 9/30/10		
☑ MNX	More					Yield 5.00%	Vol Adj +0.00%	Stock Price 200.91		
☑ IND	0 MNX					INDEX	.00	24.47%	.00	
☑ STRANGLE	SELL	-1 MNX	NOV 10	180	CALL		26.21%	2.01		
	SELL	-1 MNX	NOV 10	220	PUT	CREDIT	19.68%			

(Source: TD Ameritrade, Inc. Used with permission. For illustrative purposes only.)

Now we raise IV 5%. Notice that in fact the position does get shorter gamma, and for most traders this is all they will need to know.

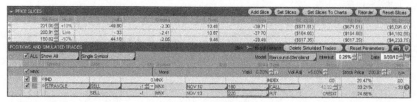

(Source: TD Ameritrade, Inc. Used with permission. For illustrative purposes only.)

However, the crazy thing with OTM options rears its head if we increase IV significantly, in this case 15%. Notice then that the gamma actually FALLS!!!

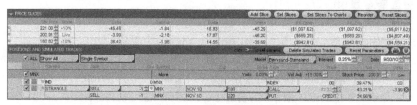

(Source: TD Ameritrade, Inc. Used with permission. For illustrative purposes only.)

Why does this happen? When IV increases, OTM options go through a progression. As IV increases, at first OTM options gain gamma as they become more like an ATM option (remember ATM options have the most gamma). Once these options gain enough IV that they actually BECOME so similar to ATM options, they begin losing gamma with increases in volatility.

While this can seem confusing, think about it this way. Way-out-of-the-money options gain gamma with increases in volatility, until they are no longer way-out-of-the-money options.

Why Do I Need to Weight My Option Portfolio?

Mark Sebastian wrote the following in his OptionPit.com blog on 12/29/2010:

> Deep down I am a floor trader at heart. This is why I get so fired up when I see traders trading without understanding the concept of weighting that I am about to run through.
>
> When I was a floor trader, the group I worked for traded SPX, SPZ, ES, DJX, DIA, and many other index options against each other. Needless to say, this was a complex process. In order to really make these trades work properly, we had to "weight" the delta and the gamma. Meanwhile, with vega and theta we had to do very little when combining the Greeks of several products (there were a lot of other things to manage with vega, but practically nothing for theta). Why would we need to do a bunch of work for delta and gamma and practically nothing for vega and theta? The answer lies in the definition of a delta.
>
> A delta represents the correlation to the underlying product for a 1-point move. The 1-point move is the important word in that statement. A 1-point move can mean different things to different underlying products. If IBM goes up one dollar, would a trader notice that it was up? Probably not! If Ford rallies one dollar, would a trader notice that? Yes, of course the trader would. For IBM $1.00 is barely more than .5%; in Ford it is closer to 6%!! A one-dollar move in IBM means a lot less to the shareholder than a 1-point rally in Ford.
>
> Why does this matter? It matters because most traders are taught to think in percentages (and most strategies are designed that way). What if I had a portfolio where I thought Ford was going to outperform IBM (I know, it would be a weird portfolio). If I sold 100 shares of IBM and bought 100 shares of Ford in my "pairs" trade, then Ford rallied 5% and IBM rallied 2%, would I make money? NO, I would be a huge loser:
>
> **F Return:**
>
> $100*16.75*.05=+83.75$

IBM Return:

$-100*146.52*.02=-293.04$

Congrats to me on being right; boo to me for not understanding how to weight these stocks according to price. If I wanted this trade to really work, I would have needed to buy about nine shares of F for every one I sold in IBM (that strategy would make $460.00). This concept is even more apparent in what we were doing when converting SPY to SPX.

When the SPX rallies 1.00, how much of an effect on the index is it, based on the reaction from traders today, when the SPX rallied less than 2.00? NOTHING! In the SPY, though, 1.00 is not an insignificant move in the underlying, amounting to about .8% (to about .08% in the SPX). Because of these, we knew that if I sold 1000 SPY calls that had a delta of 30, there was no need to panic; it was the equivalent of selling 100 calls in the SPX.

So when we were converting OEX and SPX, we would be trading about 2.23 OEX for every SPX; in DIA it was more like 11, in SPY a little under 10, and so on. Regardless of risk beta, understanding the size of the contract's underlying was a key to having a balanced portfolio. So traders, remember, in trading, size does matter!!

Gamma Scalping

Mark Sebastian wrote the following in his OptionPit.com blog on 10/27/2010:

> I get asked all the time, **"How should I scalp gamma?"** It is a surprisingly difficult question to answer. As a market maker I had very few constraints on my trading activity. I could hedge a back spread any way I wanted. If I wanted to hedge by selling stock, that was simple. I pulled up my stock execution system and unloaded the underlying. If I wanted to trade options against the gamma, I could trade just about any option in the spectrum. If I thought there was more edge in trading the January 2012 month to hedge a front month back spread, I would.

If I wanted to hedge calls with puts, or puts with calls, that was also not a problem. Retail traders lack the ability to trade and execute many hedging strategies. I soon realized it really doesn't matter what the trader uses to hedge. It matters *how* the trader hedges. While there are endless options to scalp gamma, there are two ways I teach students. One method is for very active traders that I call *"pay the decay,"* and the other is for less active traders that I call *"delta/gamma ratio hedging."*

Pay the Decay

When I first started teaching gamma scalping, the only method I taught was *"pay the decay."* This is an intense and involved form of scalping and is probably more useful for full-time traders than retail traders. All traders should understand the technique.

The trader uses theta of the position to calculate his daily "nut." The trader uses the formula for change in slope to calculate how movement is needed in the underlying to *"pay the decay."*

Looking at the blind straddle on 10/16/09, the position is long 8.25 gamma and short 6.09 theta. The trader would plug in 7/5*6.09 as the solution (7/5 to take the weekend decay somewhat into account), and use the gamma as the change in slope for the curve. The variable the trader is solving for is the change in price. The formula ends up looking like this:

$$7/5 * Theta = 0.5 * Gamma * X ^ 2$$

Or solving for X:

$$X = SQRT (7/5 * Theta / 0.5 * Gamma)$$

Which reduces to:

$$X = SQRT (2.8 * Theta / Gamma)$$

Solving the equation in this case:

$$X = SQRT (2.8 * 6.09 / 8.25) = \$1.43767$$

The SPY needs to move $1.44 in order to cover the theta decay for that day. This formula has to be rerun every morning as decay and gamma change (both get larger every day). A major complaint is that anyone who has a "real job" may not feel like doing this calculation daily. There is a much bigger problem with this formula though:

It doesn't answer when to adjust.

Most of my students assume that they should set the scalp $1.43 from the previous day's closing price. Not the case! Setting the scalp that far will only get hit about once every 3 days.

Personally, I set my scalps at 50% of the required move, and sell all of my deltas at that point. Then I buy them back when the stock moves back to unchanged. This creates two scalps that equal 72 cents of movement. I have to make this type of scalp twice, either round tripping the underlying moving 72 cents twice, or getting a combo of round trips to the upside and the downside.

At day's end, I always zero out deltas.

If the underlying "gaps" past the required move, I would sell all of the position's deltas (or at least 75% if I think the move could continue).

If the underlying hits a scalp and continues to run in that direction, I use the scalping point as my new starting point. This method requires a lot of work and can be very frustrating when the underlying really runs (I'll be honest, if I sense momentum I will let the underlying run and set trailing stop orders instead).

This type of scalping will certainly cover a portion of my decay and surprisingly is far more likely to cover my decay then setting the scalps $1.43 apart.

Why? Volatility predicts price movement, not direction.

Scalping gamma at closer intervals, I end up making far more scalps than setting the scalps further apart. When I was on the floor, trading Sun Microsystems, there were times when I would scalp 10 to 30 times in a day. By the end of the day I could have thousands of dollars in my pocket, even if SUNW (the old symbol) didn't move. One of the neat things about long gamma is that the trader wants to get in as many scalps as possible. This method allows for that.

The *"pay the decay"* method is very involved because of the large number of trades. On top of that, gamma and theta are constantly changing. Traders who can't sit in front of a computer all day have a serious problem.

As a mentor I wanted to be able to help my students trade straddles and scalp gamma if they wanted to. I asked myself, "How can a retail trader trade a straddle?"

This brought me back to my floor trading days. At any given time, I could be managing as many as 60 positions.

I had about ten stocks that were my bread-and-butter stocks. These were consistently busy. Then there were usually about five to ten other stocks that would heat up from time to time (these rotated). For the slower forty stocks, I did not have the time to sit there and scalp gamma back and forth based on the "pay the decay" formula. I actually had a different method for very small positions.

Depending on how hectic the market was, and the individual stock was, I would trade the security on a **delta/gamma ratio**. For, most stocks, I would trade them one to one.

Essentially, **when my delta equaled my gamma, I would flatten my deltas**.

At first this may seem a little arbitrary, but once you think about it, maybe it's not. The Greeks are all interrelated. When one Greek, in this case delta, clearly becomes the dominant Greek, it intuitively makes sense to cut that risk down. (It works out in the model but I will spare you guys the proof.)

Trading the delta/gamma ratio accomplishes this, without forcing the trader to sit and stare at the trader's computer.

In the morning, you can move the price up until the delta equals the gamma, then set a price alert there, and then do the same on the downside (if the trader is using stock instead of options, he or she may consider resting a small stock order there). For smaller positions or stocks that tend to trade with a momentum, I suggest that you use a somewhat larger ratio, because of commissions or to take advantage of the stocks' momentum.

Gamma scalping is really not for most retail traders unless they have a VERY strong understanding of the mechanics and the trader has clear reasons why he or she wants to get long premium in that underlying.

However, proper implementation can:

- Reduce P&L volatility
- Reduce the pain of theta decay. This allows you to stay in the position longer while you wait for your position to work.

Obviously I am back trading, but I did my best not to Monday-morning quarterback and put the scalps in where they go. Because of the size of this position, I went with a ratio of two to one. I still ended up making several scalps using puts and calls. One thing you should note:

If you are using options to scalp gamma, no matter what month the straddle is placed, the front month options should be used to hedge.

Why?

Because they have the most "pure" deltas (basically, these options have the least vega). If the position is larger, deep calls and puts can be as effective as stock. In this case, the position was so small I had to use front month out-of-the-money options to trade in and out of my deltas. This is not a very desirable way to manage deltas, but I had to deal with the cards I was dealt.

So, I ended up trading in and out of diagonals. When I exited the trade, I made slightly less than that naked straddle; however, my position had far less P&L volatility and was never down as much as the naked straddle.

Trade Summary

Posn Type	Underly Symbol	Symbol	Type	Open Date	Close Date	Posn	Open Price	Close Price	Commis on Open	Commis on Close	Total Commis	Open Cost (Proceeds)	Close Proceeds (Cost)	Gain (Loss)
Comb SPY	SWGLD	O		10/16/09	11/08/09	+1								
SPY	SWGXD	O		10/16/09	11/08/09	+1								
SPY	SPYKK	O		10/20/09	10/27/09	-1								
SPY	SWGWV	O		10/27/09	10/28/09	-1								
SPY	SWGWX	O		10/28/09	10/29/09	-1								
SPY	SWGWS	O		10/29/09	10/30/09	-1								
SPY	SWGWW	O		10/30/09	10/30/09	-1								
SPY	SWGWX	O		10/30/09	11/05/09	-1								
SPY	SWGWT	O		11/05/09	11/08/09	-1	1.03	0.91	0.00	0.00	0.00	47.00	59.00	12.00

(Source: OptionVue6)

Trade Details

	Date	Time	Code	Qty	Symbol	Type	Price	Commis	Net	R	Desc
1.	10/16/09	11:00	Buy	1	SWGLD	O	4.05	0.00	-405.00	A	SPY Dec108 call
2.	10/16/09	11:00	Buy	1	SWGXD	O	3.90	0.00	-390.00	A	SPY Dec108 put
3.	10/20/09	09:00	Sel	1	SPYKK	O	0.56	0.00	56.00	A	SPY Nov115 call
4.	10/27/09	09:00	Buy	1	SPYKK	O	0.14	0.00	-14.00	A	SPY Nov115 call
5.	10/27/09	09:00	Sel	1	SWGWV	O	0.76	0.00	76.00	A	SPY Nov100 put
6.	10/28/09	15:00	Buy	1	SWGWV	O	1.29	0.00	-129.00	A	SPY Nov100 put
7.	10/28/09	15:00	Sel	1	SWGWX	O	1.78	0.00	178.00	A	SPY Nov102 put
8.	10/29/09	15:00	Sel	1	SWGWS	O	0.39	0.00	39.00	A	SPY Nov97 put
9.	10/29/09	15:00	Buy	1	SWGWX	O	0.95	0.00	-95.00	A	SPY Nov102 put
10.	10/30/09	12:00	Buy	1	SWGWS	O	0.87	0.00	-87.00	A	SPY Nov97 put
11.	10/30/09	12:00	Sel	1	SWGWW	O	1.63	0.00	163.00	A	SPY Nov101 put
12.	10/30/09	15:00	Buy	1	SWGWW	O	1.79	0.00	-179.00	A	SPY Nov101 put
13.	10/30/09	15:00	Sel	1	SWGWX	O	2.08	0.00	208.00	A	SPY Nov102 put
14.	11/05/09	15:00	Sel	1	SWGWT	O	0.28	0.00	28.00	A	SPY Nov98 put
15.	11/05/09	15:00	Buy	1	SWGWX	O	0.65	0.00	-65.00	A	SPY Nov102 put
16.	11/08/09	00:43	Buy	1	SWGWT	O	0.16	0.00	-16.00	a	SPY Nov98 put
17.	11/08/09	00:43	Sel	1	SWGLD	O	2.59	0.00	259.00	a	SPY Dec108 call
18.	11/08/09	00:43	Sel	1	SWGXD	O	3.85	0.00	385.00	a	SPY Dec108 put

(Source: OptionVue6)

16 Oct 2009 at 11:00 AM

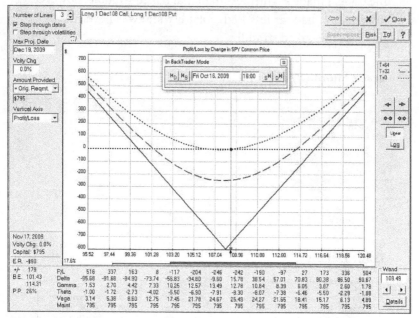

(Source: OptionVue6)

20 Oct 2009 at 9:00 AM

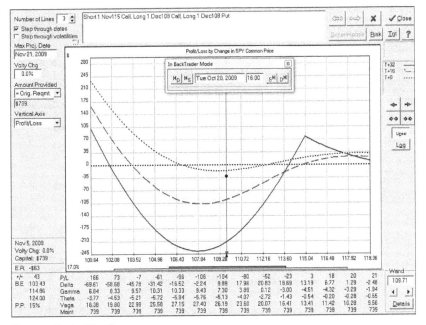

(Source: OptionVue6)

27 Oct 2009 at 9:00 AM

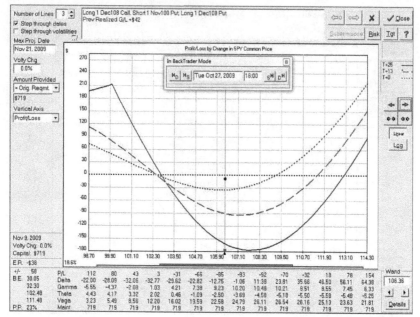

(Source: OptionVue6)

28 Oct 2009 at 3:00 PM

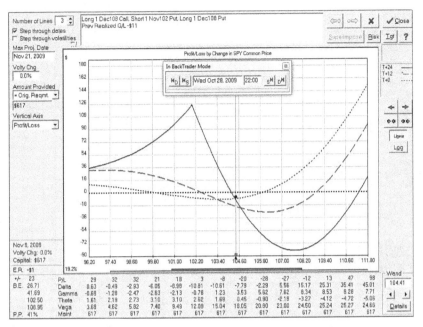

(Source: OptionVue6)

29 Oct 2009 at 3:00 PM

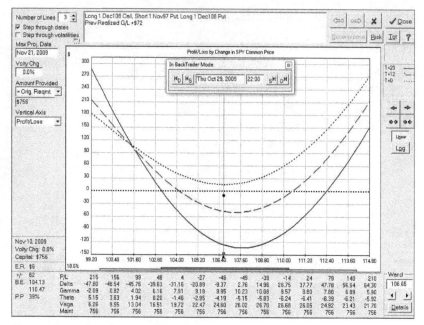

(Source: OptionVue6)

30 Oct 2009 at 12:00 PM

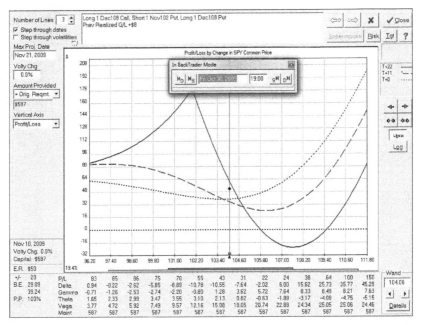

(Source: OptionVue6)

30 Oct 2009 at 3:00 PM

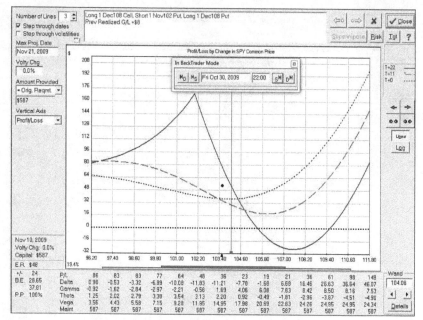

(Source: OptionVue6)

5 Nov 2009 at 3:00 PM

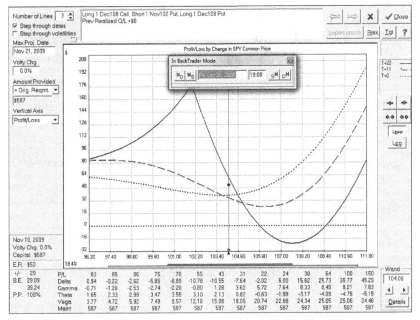

(Source: OptionVue6)

Why Do Option Trades Beta Weight Gamma, and not Theta and Vega?

Most option traders can get delta, and even the weighting factor. Gamma seems to be different; I often have new option mentoring students who do not have a full grasp of how gamma works, especially when comparing something like SPY and SPX. However, now that I have walked through delta weighting, gamma weighting should be a breeze.

Going back to SPY and SPX, we can clearly see why gamma matters in the severity of the percent movements. If SPY drops 3 dollars from 126 to 123, what percentage of a drop is that? Well, 3/126 is almost 2.5%. That is a massive one-day drop in a stock. The 126 strike would likely drop from a 50 delta to somewhere in the 30–40 delta range. That would be a change in delta of about 15 deltas a contract. Thus, the gamma would be about 5.

In SPX a drop of 3 dollars would be the SPX going from 1260 to 1257, not exactly exciting. In that process the delta of the 1260 might drop from 50 to 48.5. That would be a gamma of about .3. Same point move, very different delta effect. The reason is the percent change in the underlying. Three points in the SPX is about .25% vs. 2.5% in the SPY.

Gamma is always set for a 1-point move in the underlying regardless of the size of the contract. It might be confusing but it works, because if the SPY was down 3.00 the SPX would never be down 3, it would be down 30! Then the change in deltas actually match up:

For SPY: 3*5=15 deltas

For SPX: 30*.5=15 deltas

The gamma isn't weighted because the price movement of the underlying products is!

Vega and Theta

This will be a quick and easy one. Theta and vega are directly tied to the amount of premium in the contract, not the underlying product. It is this function that allows us to cross hedge. If I sell $3,000 of premium in SPY or SPX with 30 days to decay, then that $3,000 needs to go away in 30 days regardless of what product it was sold in. It may take more contracts in SPY, but if the premiums are the same, so should the thetas be (save the extra day of trading in SPY). Thus, theta is theta, regardless of what product it is sold in.

Because of this function, if I am short $3,000 in premium I will be short the same amount of vega or volatility exposure. Thus, if IV goes up 1 point in SPY or 1 point in SPX I will have the same loss. Thus, vega is vega, regardless of the product.

Hopefully this makes things a little clearer.

15

The Beginning

We've got news for you. This is supposed to be the final chapter, but it isn't. As Buzz Lightyear from Disney's *Toy Story* movie would say, "To infinity and beyond!" It is only the final chapter of the book, but not the final chapter in your quest to build The One Man Insurance Company. When you decide to start building your own option portfolio or hedge fund, you will never stop learning. This book is only one of many you will read on your path to becoming a successful manager in your option trading business.

To build your fund you must master all the primary and support functions of the Option Trader's Hedge Fund value chain. Make sure you understand and are able to do the following:

- Trade selection

- Risk management

- Trade execution

Also, make sure that you have in place the supporting functions:

- Trading plan

- Trading infrastructure

- A process for learning

Understand volatility and use this understanding to obtain an edge in your trades. You should be as comfortable reading volatility as you are reading the speedometer in a car. Learn all the different option strategies. Then select and use the strategies you are comfortable using. In time, like a karate master, you will master all the strategies. However, as you learn and grow, you will figure out that 80% of the time you will use 20% of your strategy arsenal. We suggest that you use vertical spreads, iron condors, butterflies, calendar (or time) spreads, and ratio spreads. These are the ones that we use the most at the Options Trader's Hedge Fund.

In Figure 15.1, we have given you the framework to set up the Option Trader's Hedge Fund as The One Man Insurance Company (TOMIC). Many of you would say that it seems to be simple enough and that it is not rocket science. But the majority would put the ideas aside and not follow through. This business is not for everyone. We appreciate that you took the time to read our book and we appreciate your support if you purchased it. If you would like to invest like TOMIC and do not want to do the work, you can look for funds that have similar investment philosophies and outsource your investment duties to them. For those of you who choose to develop TOMIC, congratulations in advance for taking the path less traveled.

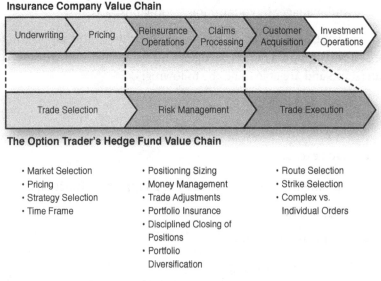

Insurance Company Value Chain

Underwriting | Pricing | Reinsurance Operations | Claims Processing | Customer Acquisition | Investment Operations

Trade Selection | Risk Management | Trade Execution

The Option Trader's Hedge Fund Value Chain

• Market Selection	• Positioning Sizing	• Route Selection
• Pricing	• Money Management	• Strike Selection
• Strategy Selection	• Trade Adjustments	• Complex vs.
• Time Frame	• Portfolio Insurance	Individual Orders
	• Disciplined Closing of Positions	
	• Portfolio Diversification	

Figure 15.1 The Option Trader's Hedge Fund value chain.

Building the Option Trader's Hedge Fund is a big endeavor. Dennis started and continues to grow Smart Income Partners, Ltd., with a lot of smart work, discipline, and commitment. Mark constantly pushes the envelope in understanding and using volatility to gain a trading edge. Be disciplined. Use the guidelines set forth in this book. Use the book as a collection of signposts marking a path. However, remember that the path never ends and that your path might not be the same as the path for others. Every reader could have a unique path because everyone has a different way of seeing the world. So your way to making money trading options might be different from ours. In fact, even we (Dennis and Mark) have different trading styles. But our goal is the same, to make money consistently.

This is the beginning of your journey, of your quest to become a TOMIC trader. Congratulations again. Never stop learning and improving your skills. Follow the path to consistent profits.

A

Recommended Reading

One of the questions Mark gets from his option mentoring students is, "What are the best books to learn options trading?" It's a good question because there are hundreds of books out there all claiming to be the best options books. The truth is, for every great options book there are nine or ten that are total junk. So here are Mark's recommended books, those that provide enough theoretical knowledge to be at the level of advanced options trader.

Category 1: The Starter

The Rookie's Guide to Options, by Mark D. Wolfinger: Yes he is a little irritable sometimes, but in the end the man cares about people. He wants to help new traders, and he wrote a pretty good beginner's book. There are other decent rookies books out there as well. *Option Spread Trading,* by Russell Rhoads, and *Options for the Stock Investor,* by Jim Bittman, are both great books as well. However, if you want to pick one, Mark Wolfinger is my choice.

Category 2: Getting Ready to Start Paper Trading

Trading Options as a Professional, by Jim Bittman: More mathematical than a beginner book, but less mathematical than an advanced book, but in the end beautifully written, highly educational, and one fine book. We have yet to find an intermediate-level book that is as high-quality as this one. He did a masterful job. One other book that we like in this class is *Options Volatility Trading,* by Adam Warner. This is probably one of the hardest areas to write in and both of these authors did it well.

Category 3: Ready to Trade

Option Volatility and Pricing, by Sheldon Natenberg: Considered by most professionals to be the bible of the industry, this is the best-written upper-level intermediate book available in the marketplace. This should be on every trader's shelf and is the closest thing to a textbook that is actually not a textbook. The other great book is Larry McMillan's *Options as a Strategic Investment.* If traders buy only one other book, I would make it one of these.

Category 4: Advanced and Mathematical

Dynamic Hedging, by Nassim Taleb: Much more nuts-and-bolts, and less preachy than his later books. If you want to understand advanced concepts of volatility, this is the source. To get any deeper means you are reading a math book. We would also suggest Jeff Augen's *The Option Trader's Workbook* at this level. It will help you apply all that you have learned.

There are several books that don't fit into any of these categories that are interesting reads; however, they make sense as supplements. Anything by Jeff Augen is worth a read. When Jared Woodard publishes, we are sure that it will be good, and parts of Charles Cottle's latest book have tremendous value. However, we would skip these until you at least get though McMillan or Natenberg.

Other Books That Might Be Useful

The following are suggestions made by Dennis to give you a wider perspective of the investment world:

> *Against the Gods: The Remarkable Story of Risk,* by Peter Bernstein. The history of risk management from its beginnings to today.

> *One Up on Wall Street,* by Peter Lynch. An investment classic on investing in equities.

> *Reminiscences of a Stock Operator,* by Edwin Lefevre. A must read for any professional trader. It is a classic.

The Inner Voice of Trading, by Michael Martin

The Tax Guide for Traders, by Robert A. Green. A good read for option and future traders who pay U.S. taxes.

Trading for a Living, by Dr. Alexander Elder

Come into My Trading Room, by Dr. Alexander Elder. Good examples of trading journals.

More Money Than God, by Sebastian Mallaby. A history of hedge funds.

The Daily Trading Coach, by Brett N. Steenbarger. A good book on trading psychology.

The CME Group Risk Management Handbook, by John W. Labuszewski, John E. Nyhoff, Richard Co, and Paul E. Peterson. This is a good reference book.

Trading in the Zone, by Mark Douglas

The Snowball: Warren Buffett and the Business of Life, by Alice Schroeder

The Paradox of Choice: Why More is Less, by Barry Schwartz

The Dhandho Investor, by Mohnish Prabai

Trend Following, by Michael W. Covel

The Intelligent Investor: The Definitive Book on Value Investing, by Benjamin Graham

Deep Survival: Who Lives, Who Dies, and Why, by Laurence Gonzales

B

Strategy Learning Sequence

Table B.1 shows a recommended sequence for learning the different strategies.

Table B.1   Strategy Development: P = Proficient, E = Expert

	Level 0 Beginner	Level 1 Intermediate	Level 2 Semi-Professional	Level 3 Professional
Long Puts	P	E	E	E
Long Calls	P	E	E	E
Covered Calls	P	E	E	E
Married Puts	P	P	E	E
Short Puts		P	E	E
Short Calls			P	E
Straddles (debit/credit)			P	E
Strangles (debit/credit)			P	E
Vertical Spreads (debit/credit)	P	E	E	E
Calendar Spreads (debit)		P	E	E
Calendar Spreads (credit)			P	E
Ratio Spreads			P	E
Iron Condors		P	E	E
Iron Butterflies		P	E	E
Diagonals			P	E
Double Diagonals			P	E
Double Calendars			P	E

You can learn all the different strategies in any order, but this is a suggested guideline of the sequence to follow based on the level of complexity of the trade. It is just like learning karate. You begin with zero skills as a white belt. Then, as you gain skills, you are promoted to different-colored belts until you obtain a black belt. However, you are not done at this point and you will never be done. There are many levels of black belts; you have just begun your training.

For a detailed description of each spread you can refer to *Option Spread Trading* by Russell Rhodes.

OptionPit.com

Option Pit provides top-to-bottom option trader education concentrating on traders who want to become full-time professional traders and traders who are already trading large amounts of capital. We are focused on helping option traders understand key trading skills and techniques, while not emptying the traders' accounts to pay for education. Students who enroll in any of our services will emerge from our program with more confidence in their ability to trade options.

We offer an array of cost-effective monthly newsletter services, educational courses, and individual courses:

1. Our Subscription service, *Option Pit Live,* provides both a newsletter service and daily market commentary. It is a combination of actionable ideas and education that every trader will find valuable.

2. Our *Silver* package is designed to introduce the basic concepts that all professionals need to know (and most retail traders do not know) within the first month of training. This introductory course will introduce concepts that even the most experienced trader may not fully understand. Silver will provide the trader with an unparalleled fundamental education.

3. Our *Gold* package is designed to provide traders with the maximum amount of education at the minimum cost. The knowledge taught in Option Pit's Gold Course is the knowledge required

by any professional trading firm. Gold is an intense, challenging, and rewarding live education course. It will put the trader in position to actively trade and not be lost.

4. The *Platinum* package includes all the education of Silver and Gold along with the one-on-one guidance traders need as they begin to trade actively. An extra three months of OP Live plus a minimum of seven hours of one-on-one time with our demanding staff will ensure that option traders are in a position to succeed without gimmicks. Traders will be able to trade any market, from calm to volatile.

5. Our *Professional Trader's Club* is designed to provide pro traders with everything they need in order to increase ROI. This is the only program on the market that focuses on using portfolio margin to one's advantage. Traders in this course are taught to think three-dimensionally when trading. This course also includes access to the Pro Trader's Club, a combination of instant messaging, weekly group meetings, and special deals on software.

Our programs focus on our three pillars that make a successful professional option trader: Trade Structure, Risk Management, and Efficient Use of Capital. Call us at **888-TRADE-01** (872-3301) or read about our Option Trader Mentoring Programs at **www.optionpit.com**.

As a special introductory offer to the purchasers of this book, OptionPit.com is offering you one month of Option Pit Live access free. Use code TOMIC1 when subscribing to the service.

D

Kite Spread

A kite spread involves the buying of a long option below where the short spread is currently placed and then selling more of the original spreads (now at a higher credit) against the long position in an attempt to pay for much of the cost of the long option. Generally, the trader's goal should be to pay for at least half of the long option in order to reduce cost. It has similar characteristics to a ratio spread, but has less vega and explosive gamma. Figure D.1 shows call credit spread and overlays the kite spread adjustment (the one that has a point like a kite at the 1390 price).

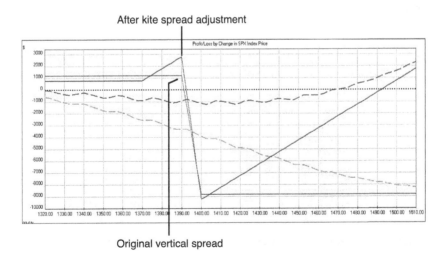

Figure D.1 Risk profile of the vertical call credit spread overlaid by the kite spread adjustment. (Source: OptionVue6)

Benefits:

The trade is long gamma, and as the underlying rallies short vega, it in many ways acts like a ratio spread.

As time passes, the trade will become longer gamma and will continue to hedge the position.

The trade is relatively inexpensive, hedges effectively, and has somewhat predictable returns.

It does not add nearly as much risk as rolling back and ramping up size.

Detractions:

There is a "sour spot" where this trade can lose money.

It adds to margin.

It does not add a lot of gamma.

Is almost impossible to execute on the downside of a condor as the spread relies on vertical skew to make the call spreads produce enough credit.

Execution:

Buy 1 call below the spread.

Sell 2-3 call spreads adding to the spread. In Figure D.2, we bought one 1370 and sold three 1390/1400 call spreads.

	MktPr	MIV	Trade	Ex.Pos	Vega	Delta
1430 calls						
1420 calls	1.70	20.5%			53.8	6.92
1410 calls	2.30	20.7%			62.0	8.27
1400 calls	3.20	21.2%	+3	+10	70.8	10.0
1390 calls	4.40	21.6%	-3	-10	80.1	11.8
1380 calls	5.80	22.1%			89.8	14.1
1370 calls	7.70	22.6%	+1		99.7	16.4
1360 calls	9.90	23.1%			110	19.2
1350 calls	12.70	23.8%			119	22.0
1340 calls	15.80	24.4%			129	25.4

Figure D.2 Kite spread trade execution. (Source: OptionVue6)

Once the trade is on, leave it on until the entire trade is unwound. It is a cheap enough adjustment; it is worth keeping on through the trade.

Index

L

M

swapping
  trades, 88
  volatility, 87
systemic risk, 37

T

tables, actuarial, 11
Taleb, Nassim, 196
Tax Guide for Traders, The, 197
tax rates, 21
TD Ameritrade, Inc., 139
term structures
  viewing, 70
  volatility, 87-88
terrorist attacks, 38
tests, stress tests, 67
The One Man Insurance
  Company. *See* TOMIC
thetas, gamma scalping, 190
ThinkorSwim, 70
Third Third Third Rule, 97
three-dimensional volatility,
  83-88
time
  to expiration, 81
  frames, trade selection, 28-29
  ratio spreads, 116
  spreads, 41, 108-114
TOMIC (The One Man Insur-
  ance Company), 2, 5. *See also*
  trades
  de-risking, 152
  exit strategies, 168-169
  functions, 17
  iron condors, 95
  learning processes, 73

management, confidence of,
  56-58
operations, 121-122
portfolio diversification, 35-36
risk management, 31, 38. *See
  also* management; risk
trades. *See also* trades
  execution, 43, 126-129
  planning, 122-124
  time frames, 28
  trading platforms, 65-67
  value chains, 14, 17
tools, analysis, 69-70
tracking volatility, 76, 88, 137.
  See also monitoring
trades
  analysis, 66
  ATM iron butterflies, 104
  bad, 34, 36
  best available, 126
  butterfly checklists, 163-165
  Card Game Value, 146-147
  coaches, hiring, 79
  delta-neutral, 52
  execution, 15-16, 43, 126-129
    designing, 48-49
    evaluating months, 46
    implied volatility, 44-46
    market conditions, 43-44
    order entry, 49-54
    product evaluations, 47
    skews, 47
    volatility, 44
  exit strategies, 168-169
  gamma scalping, 176-190
  groups, joining, 78
  holding positions, 147-149

FT Press

FINANCIAL TIMES

In an increasingly competitive world, it is quality
of thinking that gives an edge—an idea that opens new
doors, a technique that solves a problem, or an insight
that simply helps make sense of it all.

We work with leading authors in the various arenas
of business and finance to bring cutting-edge thinking
and best-learning practices to a global market.

It is our goal to create world-class print publications
and electronic products that give readers
knowledge and understanding that can then be
applied, whether studying or at work.

To find out more about our business
products, you can visit us at www.ftpress.com.